T0196832

"Emma Forrest is an incredibly gifted writer, who crafted the living daylights out of every sentence in this unforgettable memoir. I can't remember the last time I ever read such a blistering, transfixing story of obsession, heartbreak, and slow, stubborn healing."

—ELIZABETH GILBERT, author of *Eat, Pray, Love*

"Emma Forrest is as hilarious as she is wise. And did I mention generous? Unlike most memoirs this is not merely a song of oneself, but a debt of gratitude repaid to an incredible man—her psychiatrist. *Your Voice in My Head* is touching, funny, and very real."

—GARY SHTEYNGART, author of *Super Sad True Love Story*

"I read *Your Voice in My Head* in one sitting, by turns laughing out loud, gasping with recognition, and fighting to hold back tears— and wondering, of course, who *is* Emma Forrest and how is she able to write with such enormous wit and bravery about subjects most folks can't muster the courage to bring up in conversation: suicide, self-loathing, loneliness, depression, mania, and, most of all, love inexplicably lost."   —JOANNA SMITH RAKOFF, author of *A Fortunate Age*

"*Your Voice in My Head* is every drink that's ever started out sweet then turned strong enough to sneak up on you and kick your ass to the floor, or bed, or hell, or heaven."

—DAN KENNEDY, author of *Loser Goes First, Rock On,*
and host of The Moth storytelling podcast

"A brilliantly realized memoir of surprise and startling beauty."

—*Kirkus Reviews* (starred)

"[Forrest's] prose is smart and frequently witty and there are echoes of early Lorrie Moore . . . It dances along with all the lyrical panache of a novel." —JULIE MYERSON, *The Observer*

"A bittersweet love letter . . . It is a brilliant read." —*Sunday Times Style Magazine* (UK)

"Forrest's insightful and snappily written account of her lengthy battles against depression, self-harm, damaging relationships, and potato-based fried snacks is heartfelt and touching and surprisingly funny." —FLORENCE WELCH of Florence and the Machine, *Dazed & Confused*

"Forrest is stylish and evocative; whether she is sick and listless in New York or sex-dipped and radiantly happy in Los Angeles, she writes it cool, clever, and ravaging, in very few strokes . . . Her story is crushing and complicated, and entirely common . . . It's gorgeous." —KATE CARRAWAY, *Globe and Mail*

"Her style is more honest and witty than harrowing . . . It's difficult to write a convincing tale of depression that's also an entertaining romp, but Forrest has done it." —*Sunday Times*

"Describing personal experiences in a way that renders them universal, without succumbing to boastfulness, false modesty, or cliché, requires both artistry and a keen understanding of human nature. Forrest has both . . . A chronicle of different kinds of love and how they can heal the soul." —JEMIMA LEWIS, *Mail on Sunday* and *Daily Mail*

YOUR VOICE IN MY HEAD

— A MEMOIR —

EMMA FORREST

OTHER PRESS

NEW YORK

Lines from "On Raglan Road" by Patrick Kavanagh are reprinted from
Collected Poems, edited by Antoinette Quinn (Allen Lane, 2004), by
kind permission of the Trustees of the Estate of the late Katherine R.
Kavanagh, through the Jonathan Williams Literary Agency.

"Gee, Office Krupke" and "Jet Song" from *West Side Story*, words by
Stephen Sondheim, music by Leonard Bernstein © Copyright 1956,
1957, 1958, 1959 by Amberson Holdings LLC and Stephen Sondheim.
Reproduced by permission.

Every reasonable effort has been made to trace copyright holders of
material reproduced in this book, but if any have been inadvertently
overlooked the publishers would be glad to hear from them.

Production Editor: *Yvonne E. Cárdenas*
Book design: *Simon M. Sullivan*
This book was set in 12.75 pt Bembo Book by
Alpha Design & Composition of Pittsfield, NH.

LIBRARY OF CONGRESS CATALOGING-IN-PUBLICATION DATA

Forrest, Emma.
Your voice in my head : a memoir / by Emma Forrest.
p. cm.
"First published in Great Britain in 2011 by Bloomsbury."
ISBN 978-1-59051-446-7 (hardcover) — ISBN 978-1-59051-447-4
(ebook)
1. Forrest, Emma Mental health. 2. Mentally ill—New York (State)—
New York—Biography. 3. Mentally ill—Family relationships. 4. Love.
5. Psychotherapist and patient. I. Title.
RC464.F67A3 2011
362.196'890092—dc22
[B]
2010030930

Although the events described in this memoir are true,
I have changed or omitted the names and identifying characteristics of
certain individuals to protect their privacy.

This book is dedicated to:

Joe Wright (a voice on the phone)

And to Jeffrey Rosecan, his wife, and his children.

Settling his bill, he said: "There's a woman still in my room. She will leave later."

—MILAN KUNDERA, *Ignorance*

PROLOGUE

I WAS LOOKING FOR WEEKEND WORK, and though it was a Saturday job at a hairdresser's I was after, somewhere in my teenage mind I thought that Ophelia might need a hand-maiden. So, every day after school, before my mum got home, I would cycle to the Tate Gallery to visit Millais' muse.

I didn't want a Saturday job at a hairdresser's and bike riding was not my forte, but I was conscious that I was a thirteen-year-old and thirteen-year-olds ride bikes for fun and wash hair for tip money. Later I would understand that disconnect: "This is how and what I am supposed to want, and so I will try."

Approaching the Tate, I knew what was coming. I could see Ophelia's Titian hair, her white body floating down the river, the flowers around her. Sometimes, when I got there, she was dead. Other times she was still dying and could be saved by someone on the riverbank I'd never seen before. Someone Millais had sketched and then painted over, under the pigment, taking shallow breaths so as not to be seen—a man who'd let her act it out, but who wouldn't let her drown.

Though I'd never had sex, there were days when Ophelia seemed to be caught in a sexual act, her arms reached above her, her mouth open, beneath an invisible lover. A long time later—after I'd been in love—I knew that she could not let go of his postcoital scent, stronger than the smell of the flowers on the banks as she drifted by. The flowers beg her to stay in the moment. His scent keeps her locked in the past.

Those afternoons, the Tate was populated by a combination of the brightly patterned elderly and young, hip gallery patrons in black (the former keeping out of the rain, the latter longing for rain to get caught in). There was always at least one pickup going on. But mainly, on the leather banquette, in the center of the grand room, I'd sit in front of Millais' painting, eating a secret bag of crisps, and cry. Salt and vinegar was my downfall. Before the year was up I'd be rushed to hospital after eating twenty-three packets in a row. Even today, salty food—salt and vinegar crisps, marmite—tastes of regret.

I knew the painting would make me cry and yet I kept going back. I doodled her name on my notebook at school: OPHELIA, in bubble print. I wanted to be with her constantly, and when I woke up on Saturdays, I'd go there again and cry some more. I could never gauge whether I was crying for her or crying for me. It is easy to say in hindsight: I believe that she infected me. I was afraid, at thirteen, that I saw in her my own destiny.

CHAPTER 1

_____

A MAN HOVERS OVER ME as I write. Every table in the Los Angeles café is taken.

"Are you leaving?"

My notebook, coffee, and Dictaphone are spread out in front of me.

"No," I answer.

"I'll give you a thousand dollars to leave."

"OK," I say, as I pack up my things.

"What?"

"Sure. A thousand dollars. I'm leaving."

He looks at me like I'm mad and beats a hasty retreat.

I meant it. He didn't mean it. My radar, after all these years of sanity, is still off when it comes to what people do or don't mean.

My mum calls my cell phone and I go outside to take it.

"How do you pronounce Tóibin?" my mother asks me, "as in Colm Tóibin, the novelist?" This is our daily call, me in America, her in England, every day since I moved here at twenty-one. I'm thirty-two now, and she's seventy-one, though she sounds like she's seventeen.

"It's pronounced toe-bean. Like 'toe' and then 'bean.'"

"That's what I feared," she says. She lets this marinate a moment. Then, "No. Not acceptable."

"But that's his name! That's how you say it."

"I can't be going around saying 'toe-bean.' It simply will not do."

"Why don't you just not say his name?"

"He's a popular writer."

"Read his books but don't talk about them."

"No,"—I can sense her shaking her head—"some situation will arise that requires me to say his name."

I think my mother has the sense of doom, and guilt about the sense of doom, of Jews her age who weren't directly touched by the Holocaust. When she was growing up in New York, the first bad thing that happened to her was that Irish children moved into the Jewish neighborhood and stole her kazoo *and* her sailor hat. She was a fat little girl, guarding the cakes she had hidden in her sock drawer. What was a fat child in 1940s New York without her kazoo?

The second bad thing was that her dad died and then, soon after, her mother, and she was only a teenager and she didn't know how to make toast. So she got very thin—deliberately, not through lack of toast—and married a much older man. It didn't last. The best thing that happened was she fell in love with my dad.

Once, when Mum and her first husband had long since lost touch and I was new to mania, I tracked down an address for him, whom I had only heard about, and sent him a letter asking him whether or not he was dead yet. Not to be mean, just a manic need to know.

Mum gets anxious very easily. Something that is a source of calm (she watches her cat as he laps the water bowl: "Good boy, Jojo! What a good boy!") can turn, like the weather (the cat keeps lapping; her smile fades: "Why are you drinking so much water, Jojo? What's the matter, Jojo? Are you sick?").

I talk to myself a lot because I've seen her talk to herself a lot, generally in the kitchen, where she's been overheard saying, with real enthusiasm:

"I'm feeling tremendously optimistic about gluten-free bread!"

And:

"I fear George Clooney's teeth may be his downfall."

I see my mum everywhere. From certain angles, the Brazilian supermodel Gisele Bündchen has her face, and from other angles so does the black comedienne Wanda Sykes. I think all white people have a black doppelgänger and vice versa. My dad's black doppelgänger is the father in *The Fresh Prince of Bel-Air*. His Celtic doppelgänger is Sean Connery.

A lady came up to him at a hotel in Jamaica and said, "Last night we thought you were Sean Connery," and Dad said, "Last night I *was* Sean Connery."

My dad seems to know everything, so I never use Google. I only use Dad. I e-mail him a query and he figures it out, and then responds in the guise of the billionaire Google founders:

"London to Cardiff: is it expensive? How long is the trip?"

"2–3 hrs by train. Expensive if you don't book in advance. xx Larry Page and Sergey Brin."

When I was fourteen and wanting to get out of gym class, Dad wrote the teacher a letter in the shape of a perfect triangle:

to
Miss
Jensen, please
do excuse Emma from
gym today as she is feeling
unwell. Kind regards, Jeffrey Forrest

He wrote it like that for nothing but his own delight, meticulous, making me late. When I handed it to her, Miss Jensen ripped it up, threw it on the floor, and said she considered it a personal insult from my family.

He once got a credit card saying "Sir Jeffrey Forrest" because American Express was dumb enough to send him an application form with the statement "Print your name as you would wish it to appear."

The last forwarded flight details he sent me were:

YOUR SPECIAL REQUESTS	SPECIAL MEAL	REQUESTED SEAT
SIR LOVELY JEFFREY FORREST	—	12J
MS GRUMPY JUDITH FORREST	—	12K

I asked if it was really wise to ticket himself and my mother like that, and he replied, as if it were out of his hands:

"Under the new homeland security rules the ticketed names *must* be a combination of how they are printed in your passport and your likely appearance at check-in."

I like to think my parents have complementary eccentricities, two perfect jigsaw pieces of neurotica. It's all I ever wanted for myself.

I have one sister, Lisa, younger than me by three years. She had an invented childhood friend she called Poofita Kim. Her imaginary friend, as she explained in a drawing, was on the run for drowning six kids. Lisa, then five, was sheltering him. This is the same time frame in which she penned a letter to Margaret Thatcher:

> Dear Margaret Thatcher,
> Why are you so mean? The devil is not so mean. Please come to tea, Saturday, at four, to discuss your mean-ness.
> *Please wear a hat.*

I used to pour cola on Lisa's piano and take all of the stuffing out of the toy seal she slept with, so it would look like he'd deflated. Throughout childhood, she surreptitiously kept a diary of my transgressions:

3 DECEMBER 1987—Emma pulled my hair.
14 MARCH 1988—Emma poured cola on my piano.
1 SEPTEMBER 1988—When Mum wasn't looking, Emma stared at me with strange eyes, then denied that she was staring at me with strange eyes.

She's had the same boyfriend for twelve years. I haven't.

Lisa gave me *The Yellow Wallpaper* by Charlotte Perkins Gilman and sewed me underpants with a picture of Jon Stewart on them. I love her like crazy—unless Mum sets one foot in the room, and then we cannot abide each other.

My grandma is ninety and has recently adopted a Yiddish accent that creeps in when she's tired or tipsy. Otherwise she sounds just like Prunella Scales in *Fawlty Towers*, except with curse words. One year, during Wimbledon, I said I thought Stefffi Graf was attractive and my grandma shrieked, "She's an ugly bitch!" Lauren Bacall is also on her list of enemies, though the backstory remains murky.

Perhaps because my family are how they are, it took a little while to realize—settled in Manhattan at twenty-two, on contract to the *Guardian* and about to have my first novel published—that my quirks had gone beyond eccentricity, past the warm waters of weird to those cold, deep patches of sea where people lose their lives. They were in England. They didn't know I was cutting my body with razors—my arms, legs, stomach—and they didn't know I was bingeing and purging six, seven, eight times a day. Even through the darkest times, even knowing how much they loved me, I was afraid to tell them.

I was scared they'd make me leave New York, whose own eccentricity brought me the splashes of joy I still felt. Once, as I was walking on Avenue B with my friend Angela Boatwright, a bike-riding boy, of maybe eight or nine, said as he cycled past: "I'm going to fuck you in your asses!" He said it industriously, proudly, like a man with a work ethic. Later that day came the most genteel catcall I've ever received, when a construction worker yelled, "Damn, girl! I'd like to take you to the movies!"

I was incredibly lonely. I imagined accepting the construction worker's invitation and us going to the movies together, me putting my head on his shoulder and him squealing, "Eww! Get off me! I said I wanted to take you to the movies! I didn't say you could touch me!"

I did have a boyfriend—the Bad Boyfriend—and he was a huge part of the loneliness. In hindsight, I have no idea why he was ever with me. He thought highly of my breasts. And . . . that's it, I think. They were high. He didn't want to meet my parents ("I'm not really into parents"). Also on his list of dislikes:

1. Cake
2. Poetry

I really like those things. I am even quite good at making them. All I can say is: I was new in the city. I barely knew anyone. He was tall and handsome and had all his own teeth.

The first time I went to see Dr. R was in 2000, a good year to have your life turned around. I'd ridden the 6 train from the emergency room, where I had been all night. I had become so numb, in my life, that sex didn't register, unless it hurt, and then I very distantly could see that it was me on the bed. Despite the cutting and bulimia, I couldn't work fast enough to harm myself, so the boyfriend was helping out. This night he'd gone too far. Though the train car hummed with schoolkids, I felt myself in a dinghy far at sea. I could feel the blood still trickling, there in Dr. R's waiting room, as I perused an old *New Yorker*. The red staining my cotton underwear made me think of someone bleeding to death in a snowy maze, which was how I had started to feel. There was a cartoon in the *New Yorker* that didn't make sense. In the state I was in, it made me feel so lonesome, so lost and disconnected, that I started to cry. And that's how Dr. R found me, bloody and weeping, finally acting on a recommendation I'd been given months earlier.

Opening the door, like a debutante appearing at the top of a staircase, Dr. R was a slim, balding man with a turtleneck sweater tucked into corduroy trousers, belted high, which is partly why I was shocked when his wife, Barbara, told me he was only fifty-three when he died. His wisdom and his belting style: they made him seem much older.

My eyes floated around his room. The book he'd written on cocaine abuse. Three Tiffany lamps. And a framed photo of his two little boys (Andy and Sam; I'd know their names only after, from the obituary). A courtyard (open in summer unless there was too much noise from the school across the street). The best thing in the room was an art piece: a wooden cabinet of turn-of-the-century pharmaceutical medicines, including arsenic.

Dr. R settled back into his swivel chair, like a cat arranging itself on the sofa.

"You've been crying," he said.

"It was a long subway ride," I replied, assigning the blame for my tears to the 6 train, which had never done anything worse to me than roll in smelling of McDonald's.

The 6 train is also called the Lexington Avenue Line, and it has 1.3 million riders daily. It is the only line in Manhattan that directly serves the Upper East Side, running from downtown Brooklyn through lower Manhattan and finally north to 125th Street in East Harlem. It opened on October 27, 1904, and on my darkest days on my way up to Dr. R's office, I would say to myself, "A century later and this train is still running." There are twenty-seven stops and only twenty-three are in use, which humanized it somehow. As the train hurtled, averting its eyes, through the darkened 18th Street station, I imagined the 18th Street stop had simply retreated, too sensitive for life. The truth was, the new ten-car trains were too long for its platform. But I saw the pain and sadness in everything, and swirled it round my mouth like a fine wine.

After Dr. R's death, I found there were many he had saved. It's a funny feeling, like growing up and realizing that other people have read *The Catcher in the Rye*, not just you. I knew he was the director of the cocaine abuse program at Columbia-Presbyterian. I found, after his death, that he had also established a groundbreaking post-9/11 mental health program for firefighters. On the *New York Times* obituary guest book, most patients' testimonies say, "He saved my life."

During my eight years as his patient, Dr. R came to my book readings, though doctor-patient guidelines meant we couldn't talk. Still, I'd look out and see him there. His widow recently sent me a letter saying how proud he'd been of my achievements and that I held a special place in his heart. It's possible she sent letters to other patients saying "My husband really didn't like you. You bored him very badly in your sessions, largely because he thought you were beyond help. P.S.: your book was shit." But I don't think so. I know that he bought paintings by a patient who was struggling financially, and hung them in the office. I found an e-mail from 2005 asking if he could hire a sweet surfer boyfriend of mine, who he knew was trying his best to stay sober, to teach surf lessons as a birthday present for a friend's daughter.

He was cheerful. He was an eternal optimist. There was nothing I could tell him that he'd tell me was as bad as I'd decided it was. "Oh, and then I murdered a drifter. I stabbed him twenty-two times."

"Only twenty-two times? That's fewer than twenty-three."

I trusted him. And I liked how he saw me. It's that simple.

I've a mother to whom I'm so close that we sometimes have the same nightmares. I tell her everything. My dad doesn't really take things in when it comes to personal matters of great importance. One parent who loves me but doesn't listen, one who loves me but listens too hard. The point of psychiatry, as encapsulated by Dr. R, is the outside observer. The person to whom you can tell your secrets, because you will never have to face them at the dinner table.

Climbing up from rock bottom, I started going to Dr. R weekly. Then fortnightly. Then monthly. Then only as needed. My psychiatric medicine was halved in dose. I moved out to Los Angeles and we'd do phone sessions. I'd do a session in person the three or four times a year I went back to New York.

This March, I called to make an appointment when I knew I was flying to New York to meet up with a man I'd been seeing for only a few months, though it was already hard to imagine a time when we hadn't been together (he named himself my "Gypsy Husband" and I call him "GH"). I was going to tell Dr. R: "I'm in love, with someone good and kind, gentle, and he's seen the darkness too but somehow we've become each other's light. You made me well enough to be somebody's light!"

I also planned on talking to him about adjusting my meds, bringing down the dose a little more, since I'd been feeling so calm and so happy for so long. I'd even written a *Guardian* essay about my recovery from a nervous breakdown, in which I'd lavished praise on my doctor. I thought it was a little odd he hadn't e-mailed me to say he'd seen it. But I knew he was busy.

With my hotel waiting and my underwear packed, I called to make the appointment where I'd tell him my good news. I've met "The One." ("Do you mind me writing in my book that you're 'The One'?" I ask GH, typing on the porch as he makes salmon for dinner. "I'd love that," he answers, "because it means that we're 'The Two.'")

Dr. R's machine picked up but with a new greeting:

"Due to a medical issue this office is closed. This machine will not take messages."

None of his patients had a clue he was sick, let alone that he had lung cancer. He kept the truth from us for the eight months from his diagnosis up until his death, going straight from chemo to appointments. He canceled sessions because he was "feeling under the weather." Our final conversation was when I called to warn him that, as happened so many times during our time together, my check might bounce (hypermanic people: bad at handling money).

"I'm not worried about it, Emma," he said. He had maybe three weeks to live.

When I got back from visiting GH in New York, I remembered to check the e-mail set up so that readers can write to me through my website.

May 21, 2008

Emma,
I was doing a google on "Guestbook for Dr. R" when I came across an article written by you. I was very impressed by your honesty and the clarity of the article. I'm the brother-in-law of Dr. R and I don't know if you heard that he passed away two weeks ago after a nine-month fight with cancer. Yes, a truly great man and will be sadly missed by all the family. You'll find many thoughts about him by googling "Guestbook for Dr. R."

John Crawford.

Later that day, I got an e-mail from my dad. It was not in the shape of a triangle:

Mum just called and told me the sad news. I am sad because he was one of your great supporters and I know how much you loved and trusted and relied on him. I don't know who first noticed that the good die young, but it does seem to be more than a statistical anomaly.

After Dr. R died, I called that ansaphone that would not take messages, and called it again, over and over, like opening and closing the fridge door in search of food that isn't there. If I called enough times he might be. I called until, one day, it was disconnected and there was nothing on the line but my own breath.

JUNE 5, 2008

It is with great sorrow that I write these words. Dr. R rescued my son from a very serious drug addiction. He saved his life and gave him back to us.

Ever since then, for the past twelve years hardly a week has gone by without them seeing each other or speaking on the phone if my son was out of the country. Dr. R became his mentor, close friend, and life coach. He along with everyone who had the privilege of being in his care was at first horribly shocked to learn of his passing, and then completely devastated, which my son still is.

H (NEW YORK, NY)

CHAPTER 2

———————

I'M WRITING FROM MY OLD New York City apartment on the seventeenth floor. From the window I can see the hospital where I was taken after I tried to kill myself, just a few weeks after I started seeing Dr. R. With me hooked up to a monitor behind them, my mother handed him the suicide letter, which he read once, then handed back.

"I'm so sorry," he said, "I thought she was getting better."

It's important to me that my savior made a misstep at the very beginning. It humbled and humanized him in my head. Having put me on Zoloft that first, bloody day and monitored my progress, he had deemed me not a danger to myself. He was wrong.

St. Vincent's Hospital is where the ambulance men deposited me after my roommate found me unconscious. She didn't see me at first because I'd passed out in an open suitcase of yet-to-be-unpacked clothes. I hadn't unpacked it for three months. After they pumped my stomach I was put on suicide watch and a drunken volunteer nun had to come with me into the stall whenever I needed the toilet. "Jesus loves you!" she trilled. I imagined a toilet-bound Christ as Peeping Tom, all unwashed hair and heavy breathing.

When I first came to see this apartment, the view of the Empire State Building across the city felt like the moment when Richard Beymer first spots Natalie Wood across the crowded room in *West Side Story*. The rest of the city fell away. It was just us, the Empire State rising to touch the sky, me living above my means. I'm only five foot one. I looked at the building and imagined it would help keep me safe; grabbing items for me from top shelves I couldn't reach.

The MetLife Building sits, squat, to the right, like the Empire State's fat but funny best friend. I can also see the Chrysler Building, pointy and sharp as the heel on a Louboutin stiletto. I imagine a giant Carrie Bradshaw lying on her back, one shoe in the air as she cries quiet, hot tears because Big decided she was too demanding. Amazing that I ended up here, just looking out at that hospital, just another sight to be seen, me alive and looking in on it.

"You will not be pretty for husband!" scolded an Indian nurse, that dreadful March day, surveying my cuts as he inserted an IV drip into my inner elbow. I say dreadful, which it was for those who loved me, but for me there was no dread; it was as I had expected. I had looked forward to it. This was the endgame.

As they pumped my stomach, they tried to figure out if the cuts on my arm were part of the suicide attempt. They weren't. They'd been added over days and weeks and months. A graffiti artist, coming back in dead of night to a favorite wall. I self-mutilated regularly, mostly with razor blades, mostly on my arm, sometimes on my thighs, latterly my neck and face, my stomach (just once, with feeling). I started cutting when I was sixteen.

"And when did the bulimia start?" asked Dr. R, high-trousered in his leather swivel chair. His forehead was round, as if his brains were trying to leap right out and lay themselves between us, a gallant cloak to help me over my psychiatric cesspool.

"It started the day I moved to New York."

"You suddenly thought it would be a good idea?"

"Yeah. I guess. Like, how cavemen invented fire."

He laughed. He had a lovely laugh.

And it was funny. I moved to the greatest city in the world and stayed home and ate cakes. And threw them up. It was a miserable existence but I felt powerless to stop it. Bulimia is the wicked twin of orgasm. The penetration, obviously, the loss of control. It is *la petite mort*.

"Your mother thinks," he said, the Midwestern flatness of his voice making any sentence seem like hard fact, "that New York brought this out in you."

"Yes, oh yes, of course. But I think New York did it in a good way. Like the medieval use of leeches . . ."

"Bringing fever to the surface?"

There wasn't a reference point he didn't get. Musical. Cinematical. Emotional.

"Yes. I feel incredibly grateful to the city. It was always there, this sadness—I was twelve, sitting up at night, praying to die—but it had never been, you know, openly expressed before I moved here."

Dr. R swiveled. "I think we can say it was the combination of cutting and bulimia that was the speedball that triggered the event."

Event! Like event planning! I found his language made my actions less frightening.

He was right. I had stopped my daily calls with Mum. We'd always talked three, sometimes four times a day. Before the attempt, I was harder to get hold of. I was awake all night and asleep for most of the day, letting the ansaphone take her calls. When I did talk, I would be either monotone or babbling.

"You sound speedy," she'd say.

"Well, that's because I've had a brilliant idea for a film. It's called *Mrs. Dolphin*, and it's about a man who falls in love with a back massager in the shape of a dolphin."

Given how mentally divergent I sound, you might think it fantasy when I say that the top executive at Sony had flown me out to California to discuss making my debut novel into a film and to see what other scripts I might want to write. But it's true.

"That," said Mum, as I babbled about *Mrs. Dolphin*, "is not a good idea for a movie."

I was outraged. I refused to speak to her for three days. I sent in my pitch to the woman at Sony. I don't hear back.

At the same time that I've graduated from cutting my body to cutting my face, I have started to worry, terribly, about the mental health of people I have never met.

"I would prefer," says Dr. R in the week before my suicide, "that you stop sending prison packages to Robert Downey Junior."

"I just feel like I can save him and that I'm the only one. I'm sending him mix tapes of music that will help."

"Instead of sending mix tapes to Robert Downey—"

"Junior." I make this distinction as if it excuses my behavior, like, what kind of sick person would send unsolicited packages to Robert Downey *Senior?*

"Junior," Dr. R concedes, "please send them to me."

So I give him a mix tape. And I send my dad a mix tape. And then I try to kill myself.

MAY 13, 2008

I met Dr. R in college, and I remember thinking that the term "Renaissance man" seemed to apply to him more than to anyone else I knew. A pre-med student focused on art history who played ball and laughed easily, he was a larger-than-life figure, particularly because all of this intellectual and physical activity was infused with joy and optimism.

I recall only one instance of doubt, when he returned from his med-school interview a little befuddled by the fact that the entire conversation had been about art. Those of us waiting to hear how it had gone assured him that such a conversation was a really good sign, because it seemed to acknowledge what we all knew—that his enthusiasm was infectious, and that he was a well-rounded human being, not a pre-med workaholic with no interests outside of organic chemistry labs.

For Dr. R, life was filled with joy in the present and hope for the future. Yet he was not naive. He was a face-the-facts realist and bemused skeptic. His confidence in the future was rooted in a firm belief that it took an effort to make hope real.

Twelve years after we graduated from college, Dr. R responded to a friend's call for help and helped save my life. He acted swiftly, with grace and calm—and that ever-present unerring devotion to hope. I was never Dr. R's patient, but I am alive today because he was my friend.

B (NEW JERSEY)

CHAPTER 3

ON FIRST MOVING TO THE CITY, I live on Bleecker and 11th Street. In later years, the block will be destroyed by three Marc Jacobs stores, a Ralph Lauren, and the Magnolia Bakery (which we call "Studio 54 the Bakery" because the lines are so long, they have security on the door to moderate crowds). But in 2001 Magnolia is sparse, especially in the morning when I eat my daily breakfast bun, a cake in disguise. Magnolia has coffee like muddy tears, but it gets me out of the house. Next door are the Moondog Café and a psychic shop. There's an ill-lit florist where the owner shrieks, "I shall create you a bouquet such as Gianni Versace might have made for a favorite niece!" There's a bookstore, Biography, where they dress their golden retriever as Marlon Brando for Halloween. (He has a white V-neck T-shirt with Marlboro rolled into the sleeve. He doesn't shout "Stellllaaaa!" but he does have a baleful bark.)

Bad Boyfriend likes to eat late night at the Moroccan restaurant on Avenue B. On our first date I notice, when he hangs it, that his jacket is Helmut Lang, and he notices I have a gold nameplate necklace that says PRINCESS. I don't feel like a princess. Or rather, I feel like a zaftig and uncomfortable, trapped princess. A White House–era Chelsea Clinton. Since I'm a cat who doesn't know what I am, I wear track pants with old-skool Nikes but Gina Lollobrigida skintight sweaters. I am caught between childhood and va-va-voom. My dark hair is pixie cut, with little wisps of blond and orange at the tips. I'm trying to look like Roxy, my old tortoiseshell cat from childhood. I'm trying to look like a dead cat. I'm trying to look like an elderly movie star no one cares about anymore. I was trying to figure out what the hell I looked like. I envied women with signature hairdos, signature perfumes, signature sign-offs. Novelists who tell *Vogue* magazine: "I can't live without my Smythson notebook, Pomegranate Noir Cologne by Jo Malone, and Frette sheets." In the grip of madness, materialism begins to look like an admirable belief system.

Because of this, I think Bad Boyfriend really has his life together. The only love letter he ever sends me says:

> If I could buy all the Prada stores in the world, it wouldn't express how strongly I feel about the little bear who somehow got lost in this big world.

He doesn't matter, in the end, Bad Boyfriend. I don't have his number in my special tin: I have the pieces of paper on which the Big Three wrote their numbers the night we met. I was with each of them from the instant we met. Bad

Boyfriend was, instead, a product of that ugly American thing—dating—romance as a branch of accountancy.

On that first date, I burn my tongue on couscous and spit it into his hand. He looks like he might pass out. And yet we keep dating. He gives me pot one night and I inhale for the first time and am a zombie for twelve hours. I remember, in his railroad apartment, his roommate the other side of an IKEA curtain, Bad Boyfriend undoing my top and looking, just looking at my breasts, touching and squeezing them. Then he forces me to go out and eat something. I take one spoonful of soup and then lie on the floor of the Moroccan café and vomit. Lots. He drags me to my feet and I throw up on someone's dinner plate. On our way out he hands me a psychic's flyer from the restaurant's community pinboard that says "If You Need an Angel." It is sweet. I still have it. The gesture was sweet. Bad people very often do one good thing. In my memory, that gesture was Bad Boyfriend's miniaturized version of Nixon and China.

Other things I still have: lots of photobooth strips.

Because I've started to feel I'm not long for this world and because I'm fascinated by my newly prominent ribs. I am aware that I am dying. On another coast, though I haven't met him yet, my Gypsy Husband is beginning his descent.

There are still many reasons to stay awake, mainly humans, who metaphorically slap me into consciousness at various points during the day. There is Teeter, who has pink hair, green eyes, and a fetish for the teen adventure film *The*

Goonies. She stands on the fire escape, quoting from it, like a Shakespearean soliloquy:

"Don't you realize? The next time you see sky, it'll be over another town. The next time you take a test, it'll be in some other school. Our parents, they want the best of stuff for us. But right now, they've got to do what's right for them. Because it's their time. Their time! Up there! Down here, it's our time. It's our time down here. That's all over the second we ride up Troy's bucket!"

Her connection to the movie is so strong that she will eventually move to the town in Oregon where it was filmed. For now, she lives in the building next door. We can climb into each other's bedroom from our mutual fire escape. In New York City, a mutual fire escape feels infinitely more profound than a mutual orgasm.

Of my other friends, there is Bianca, a beautiful Chilean from Queens who loves Run-DMC and the Ramones equally. She shops compulsively for baby clothes. (Ten years later, after myriad miscarriages, she will have her first child. She will buy all new clothes.)

Angela fights people who aren't metal enough, who wear Motley Crüe shirts because they're trying to be cool and not because they really care about Motley Crüe.

Shannon is a holistic chiropractor who can do healing energetic work on you whilst simultaneously drinking a mojito and reading *Us Weekly*.

Sarah Bennett, aka SB, has a plush stuffed doll of Frida Kahlo on her sofa and a photo of Eudora Welty above her bed. SB and I are very different people. The best example I can give is our divergent reactions the time we were in the ice-cream aisle of Whole Foods and "Rhythm Is a Dancer" came over the piped music. SB ran out, mortified, dumping her shopping. I stayed behind and danced. One day we went into a public restroom and someone had done a poo *on the toilet seat* and when I saw it, I screamed and half-fainted and SB had to carry me home.

Peter lives next door. He is a skateboard photographer. He comes over to kill things for me. What kind of things, I cannot tell you—I just hear them scurrying in my mess of old newspapers piled through my apartment, and I run for his door.

Karen is a friend of Bad Boyfriend's from childhood and he doesn't want her anymore so I take her because she's smart and kind and funny and deeply, profoundly needy and nobody wants her, not even her own family, and it breaks my fucking heart.

Several of my mum's college roommates are in New York. I have the aforementioned family. I have so many places to turn. But anytime I go to see my family I barely talk and then I have to excuse myself to lie down for a while.

I often go to Century 21, the discount clothes store located at the World Trade Center, because it opens at 7 a.m. and I have too many hours to kill. I float from room to room and engage opinion from women in the communal changing room. I buy things, partly because I just want a reason to talk and partly because, even in terrible depression, I am unable to say no to wholesale prices.

Bad Boyfriend and I finally break up and I go, crying, to Shopsins, which has since moved. It was a diner on the corner of Morton and Bedford streets. The cantankerous owner, Kenny Shopsin, would throw people out if he didn't like them/their attitude/their face. Every day I would eat his egg-and-cheese enchilada concoction called "Blisters on My Sisters." It was mad. Everything was mad. There was no context to my madness because everyone was bonkers. But they were all functional and I didn't realize that I wasn't. "You're like Marilyn Monroe," Kenny tells me, which I take as a compliment and say a nervous "Thank you." Interrupting, he adds, "You're all velvet and velcro. Men want you because you're sexy and broken and when it gets too tough they can say 'Hey! This toy is broken!' and toss you aside without feeling bad."

This makes me sadder than anything I've ever heard.

I go to a soul-food restaurant called the Pink Tea Cup at night to fill the hours I'm awake, so I won't feel lonely. I eat pecan pancakes. Breakfast all day is like hope. A fresh start at midnight. The jukebox is amazing and I come to know which are the longest songs available for my quarter. It has Roy Ayers's "Everybody Loves the Sunshine," Donny Hathaway's cover of "Jealous Guy," "Living for the City" by Stevie Wonder. It's a freezing February. The night-shift cook and the waitress at the Pink Tea Cup let me join their game of Boggle.

I think the fact that New York has numbered streets keeps me alive for a long time. Just keep walking. Just keep moving. As much as I cut myself, there is also pain and achievement, elation, of course, in pounding the pavement. 11th to 86th. 1st Ave. to 10th.

I listen to "The River" by Bruce Springsteen, over and over. I think of Ophelia. I can feel the weight of her soaking clothes with every step.

Mania flows like a river approaching a waterfall. Depression is a stagnant lake. There are dead things floating and the water has the same blue-black tinge as your lips. You stay completely still because you're so afraid of what is brushing your leg (even though it could be nothing because your mind is already gone). That's why you lie in your bed (in the center, with my dark blue sheets. The silver curtains are a nod to mania. They were something that seemed like a good idea at the time). My bras are hung on the wall behind my bed, crucified for my sins. I have thirty-six bras. I counted. I hold my hands over my breasts in my days and weeks and months in bed, as if someone might steal them.

Though I don't even live in a one-bed (I live in a studio; it has a wall built through the center to give the illusion of two rooms), I take a roommate. I don't remember why I take a roommate. Maybe I know I should be watched. But she is very rarely there because her life is so full. She is always busy being free.

Another English girl in New York, she has a signature hairdo (bleached white-blond piled on top of her head) and a catchphrase ("Love it!"). Her curiosities are all over my apartment. Incredibly expensive shoes. A hot pink inflatable guitar. Handbags to fit a Mary Poppins coat stand inside.

I am very, very thin. I soon find that when I no longer have to dress to flatter my curves, I wear turquoise leopard-print tights under a pajama romper, with high-top Converse, or tights with thigh-high stockings with denim cutoffs and ballet slippers that have Smiths lyrics scrawled on them. People stop me in the street. For the first time in my life, I am fashionable.

Then, a couple of things happen. Skateboard Peter is not there to kill a water bug. Pounding the pavement looking for him, I run into a writer I admire who has enthusiastically blurbed my book. "Hey, I'm Emma Forrest."

"Oh, hey, Emma."

"Thanks for the blurb."

"I really liked the book."

I pause. "Can you come upstairs and kill a water bug for me?"

He looks at me like I am a water bug. "No."

"No?"

"*No.* I'm not getting involved in your life."

Then a girlfriend takes me to the movies, bringing along the paralyzingly shy comedian Garry Shandling. Afterwards I notice his shoelaces are untied. My focus is off everywhere, looking at the corners of people, not their eyes. Sometimes their mouths. With sadness comes a staring problem. Without saying a word to him, I bend to tie his shoelaces. Laces tied, he runs away, fast. My friend is upset. I am so crazy, I am crazier than a comedian.

The third thing that happens is I run into Sam, a friend of a friend who has wanted me forever. I wasn't really interested and I had a boyfriend. Now I have no boyfriend and I go to parties alone. I tell him I am single. "So you can kiss me."

"No, thanks," he answers. He looks at me and then at the floor. "I don't want to anymore."

Fourth and final, I go to see *Ghost Dog*, the Jim Jarmusch film about an urban samurai, starring Forest Whitaker. Only I would allow Forest Whitaker to take such a pivotal role in my decision to die. When he wins his Oscar many years later, I say to the screen, "I want the seven grand you made me lose to St. Vincent's Hospital, you bastard!"

Do not try to kill yourself without insurance, because if you survive, you will be in so much debt, you will want to die. This becomes a big deal with Dr. R. Because of what I have done, I cannot afford to see him. He drops his fee and keeps it there until the very last year of our sessions.

Before my suicide note, there is a pre-suicide note, an aperitif if you will. I send my dad a strip of photobooth portraits stuck to a piece of paper that says "Emma loves Daddy."

I have no memory of sending it.

Dad's response arrives after I'm out of hospital, sent before he knew I was headed there. He photocopies the picture and then turns the photos upside down and draws himself—his beard, his bald head—onto my face, adding: "And Daddy loves Emma."

CHAPTER 4

I FIRST THOUGHT OF IT at thirteen. We had a large bathroom
with a wall-to-wall mural of peacocks and birds of paradise,
jungle birds and tall grass, inspired by Gauguin. I also had
a mural in my bedroom: my dad had helped me paint in
huge letters on my wall: D.A.I.S.Y., which stood for Da
Inner Sound Y'all, the motto of the hip-hop group De La
Soul, the first band I loved. They had a skit at the start of
their album *3 Feet High and Rising* with a fake game-show
host asking a fake game-show audience nonsense questions:
"How many feathers are on a Perdue chicken?" "How many
fibers are intertwined on a shredded wheat biscuit?" "What
does toosh et leh leh pu mean?" "How many times did the
Batmobile catch a flat?" "We'll let the contestants think it
over and we'll return right after these messages!"

Because of the glorious mural, the bathroom became
more of a family hangout than the living room. Many con-
versations took place whilst Dad was in the bathtub, bub-
bles and a fancy newspaper holder covering his dignity as

he read the *Independent*. Mum would be at the mirror using what looked like a heated light saber to turn her head of curls from wee ethnic ringlets to chubby glamour rolls. Lisa would be stalking the room, saying "It's not *fair!* It's not *fair!*" because, even though she was nine, she functioned primarily as Guardian of Justice. I remember, in the bathroom, at far too late an age, eating a bar of soap in the shape of *The Muppet Show*'s Fozzie Bear, because I loved him and so I wanted to consume him, even if it made me ill. I didn't yet know the word "foreshadowing."

It was in the sacred family meeting place that I one day turned the brass key in the door and climbed up onto a chair to reach the shelf in the wooden cabinet that held Mum's Valium. Staying balanced on the chair, I tipped out the pills and held them in my hand, weighed them, as if they had wisdom to impart. I couldn't hear them speak, so I put six of them on my tongue and held them there, waiting for the message. Didn't swallow, but waited to die, or to half die, for a few minutes. I didn't die. I spat them out. I put them back in the bottle. Replaced the cap. Gingerly turned the key. And went downstairs for dinner.

It's almost always pills with women. It's a gentle seeping out women seek, like on a classic soul record, when the volume on Otis Redding just slowly gets turned down until he's gone. What happens after the fade-out? What are the musicians doing now in that room? *Take me there. Take me there.*

CHAPTER 5

_____

MANHATTAN BEARING DOWN ON ME, I walk home from *Ghost Dog*, hand in hand with the thought of suicide. The thought of suicide is masculine energy, with manicured nails, like a mafioso. It wears a warm jacket that it drapes across my shoulders, and it doesn't feel the cold itself. Do you remember the scene in *Goodfellas* where Robert De Niro keeps telling Lorraine Bracco, "There's a dress for you in that warehouse room. That one. Go on. Just go in there"? And she knows she's about to be killed, so she doesn't go in there? The thought of suicide tricks you in there with sweet talk, and even though you know you're being sweet-talked, and you know what lies in store for you, it's a room you want to go to anyway.

The well-groomed Thought of Suicide holds the door to my building for me. In the warmth of my apartment, we pick up my razor and cut together, like taking friendly shots in a bar. *L'chaim!* I look again and TOS is a manager taking me through important documents as I draw the blood from my skin with a razor pen. "Sign here. And here. And once more, here."

The Thought of Suicide is a big flatterer. "You're very pretty," it says, and I blush but I also believe it, the light of the thought bleaching out my imperfections. Later GH will say, "You're a great shag and very beautiful, but you don't care about such things," and internally I laugh and laugh because I think it is my vanity the Thought of Suicide played hardest on.

I lie down on the bed. There are papers all over the queen-size mattress, books, newspapers, a bottle of water, pills. Pills tucked in there already, just waiting, just more. The pills begin to kick in. This is very pleasant, I think, like the moment you step into a warm bath, or the moment he slides inside you for the first time.

And then the tide pulls back and there are things on the sea-bed I didn't know were there: rusty cans, empty Coke bottles, seabirds choked in plastic. And it isn't pleasant anymore.

Somewhere in there is a bell, maybe a child playing a triangle. I reach for the triangle to make it stop. It's the phone. "Hello," I say from the ocean.

It's my mother. "Emma? Emma? EMMA! What have you done?"

How does she call an ambulance? She doesn't. I have dropped the phone and wandered into the suitcase to pass out and am now unconscious. She hears my roommate walk in. Mum is still there and hears everything. She hears my roommate scream. She hears her call 911 on her cell. She hears the ambulance men arrive. She stays there. She doesn't go anywhere. My mum is here with me, for all of it.

Eventually she hangs up to book a ticket so she can fly to be with me that evening. She flies through the night and I fly through the night and the next day we are in a hospital room together. I peel open my sticky lids. An IV leads from my arm to a drip. I'm in a bed and she's on a chair and there's someone else there with us—suicide watch—is it the Haitian or is it the drunken volunteer nun those first hours?

E-mail to Dad from Mum:

Subject: This and That.

It's midnight my time and I've been cleaning for several hours just so that I could breathe. Nothing changes.

At the moment, nobody quite knows what to do about Emma. Tomorrow morning she will be assessed by the psych resident at St. Vincent's. They may want to keep her but I think I will try to get her out. I don't know what it's costing but I will find out for certain tomorrow morning. They don't know her, they're going by the rules, and I'm not impressed. I'm much more interested in her being assessed by her own therapist and by the pharmacologist who has prescribed her meds which seem to have helped over the past eighteen months. We want to get some fix on what caused this. I'll know more during the day tomorrow.

She is insisting that she must get on with her work. She's physically OK.

It might be good if you can find out something from AMEX insurance—possibly, we might get away with saying that she had a psychiatric incident, as long as we bring her back to the UK. They certainly won't cover any extended treatment.

Other than that, please remember the garbage and freeze what needs freezing. I will probably stay until Sunday and use the flight you booked.

I forgot my ear plugs.

Love from me and from Emma too.

Whilst the hospital keeps me, friendless Karen takes Mum to dinner at the Pink Tea Cup. I know Karen is grateful to be of service. She is like someone who loves fire, helping to put out a fire.

MAY 2008

Your father/husband helped to get me sober. He was a good, good man. I'm so sorry.

DOUGLAS (NEW YORK, NY)

CHAPTER 6

FOR A FEW DAYS after I'm out of the hospital, I'm completely lucid. I'm cheeky and brimming with joie de vivre. It's not gratitude. I have successfully altered my mood. For a spell.

SB and Teeter stick by me. But I lose a number of friends over the suicide attempt.

"It's understandable," says Dr. R. "They're frightened. It's a frightening thing to do."

I don't understand why I've been disinvited from parties. I am not seeing the big picture.

Afterwards, you can't just fall back into life like someone appearing at the door wearing a monocle and top hat, saying, "Hullo! I was just in the neighborhood following my failed suicide attempt and I thought I might stop in for a cocktail!"

"Are you surprised that people might not want to see you?" Dr. R asks me.

"I think they're jealous. It's something they've thought about. But I did it."

"This isn't exactly an achievement."

"No. I failed."

The ones who use the suicide to draw closer are loners on the edge, peering from their abyss into yours. Karen calls constantly.

Dr. R wants to send me to Silver Hill, the Connecticut rehab/psych facility. But being one of America's forty-four million uninsured, I can't cover the thirty grand. If we go for an assessment and they deem me a danger to myself they will commit me anyway and I will have to find the thirty grand or face legal action. We decide to go back to London, although there really isn't any decision; Britain's National Health Service is the only option.

I think this should be the new campaign of the British Tourist Board: "England: when it's the only option."

Mum goes ahead of me to look into available treatment in the land of "Oh, do pull your socks up!"

I arrive at the airport with hand luggage. My parents aren't there. Dad has made them late, because he is afraid, Mum thinks. So there I am waiting at Heathrow arrivals, no idea where my family is, and I can't remember how to use a pay phone. I don't understand English money anymore. I can't remember my parents' phone number. I sit on the floor of the airport and cry. Crying makes the cuts on my neck swell. When my parents arrive, my dad is chastened. He can't look at me.

I go back to their house. As I recall, I climb into bed and Mum's cats come to comfort me. But that's not true because our cat, Roxy, died ten years ago, and Mum is not allowed cats until years later, when Lisa persuades Dad they are a good idea. So there is nothing crawling on me but my own anxiety.

Mum is figuring how I can get help as an outpatient somewhere, until, waking on my first morning home, I have a nice cup of tea and then destroy the bathroom. Outpatient no longer seems so viable. I tore that room apart. I wrote on every wall. I got words written up on the ceiling. How? When you're losing your mind you can manage the same unthinkable feats as a very drunk person. I don't know how I got to the ceiling. I did it in a fever dream and was shocked when it was over, to see what I had done. Mum is terrified. "Your father's going to go crazy!" When you're unhinged, you make others unhinged. It's like watching someone yawn. It's catching. But that isn't what happens. Dad comes home from work early. He silently examines the room, as if it were an art installation. Then he comes out, crying.

"It's just objects."

He wraps his arms around me.

"How can we help you? What should we do?"

I love him so much. But: "I don't know."

It's by now very hard to get words out at all. I'm in a trance. Someone with deep spiritual awareness might be in such a trance as I, who am so deeply lost. That night at a restaurant dinner, I hold my arm on the scalding hot radiator to try to feel my way back into my skin, call my body back to me (the burns I make are my Bat Signal in the sky). But I don't come back to me. And I'm taken to the hospital the next morning.

I don't recall how we got to the Priory (again, like a drunk or a patient recovering from anesthesia, you remember the where but not the how). I clearly remember being admitted by a Chinese nurse who became affronted when I answered his questions in monotone.

"Why she not want talk to me? Why she don't like me?" he asked my mother.

"Um, she just tried to kill herself."

He storms out in a huff and a new nurse comes to finish for him.

Just sign here, they tell my mother.

And she does.

I have officially been committed, pending reevaluation.

I haven't been home to London in a long time, before being forced back, and my visitors are few and far between. And random. The closest friends can't face it. The acquaintances I've held at a distance see it, maybe, as a way to get to know me, although there is currently no "me" to know.

Matthew—"Handsome Matthew," a boy I knew when I lived in Brighton—brings me a McDonald's belt he found in the trash, and a copy of *Against Nature* by Joris-Karl Huysmans. Andrew—I don't recall his last name, but I know we went on a date once and I stole a T-shirt from his skateboard store and he drank Goldschläger in St. James's Park—brings me a Bruce Springsteen and the E Street Band sweatshirt from a charity shop. Even though I can't remember his last name, I still wear the sweater all the time. There is a hole over the "E," which is over my heart. He knows (I must have told him on our one date) how much I love Bruce Springsteen. I admire the lad for pursuing his crush to a mental ward.

I play "Human Touch" by Bruce and his wife, Patti, on my Walkman at night: the line about a little touch-up and a little paint takes me to a time when, after school, as a very little girl, I would ritually lock myself in the bathroom and cover my face in makeup, starting expertly—sharp eyeliner, dainty lips—before devolving soon enough into evil clown face. I'd take a good look at the terrible face. Then I would wash it all off and go downstairs for dinner. I can see the line from there to cutting. Before the cutting but after the face paint, when I would learn a bad word, I would write it on my thighs or stomach and wear it to assembly under my school clothes. "Fuck." "Cunt." "Whore." School assembly was frightening because I was so sure I would stand up and shout the words I had on my skin.

There are much crazier people than me in the Priory. The dog-woman, who stares. I always thought Joan Crawford was a great movie star because she made staring her hallmark, her "thing." This old lady is more like Eddie, the dog from *Frasier*. She just stares at people as they come into her sightline. It's all she does.

There's a very sexy teenage girl who, to stop cutting herself, plucks each and every hair off her legs and then wordlessly, without realizing, leans over and plucks my eyebrows. My cats do this, diligently licking themselves until they are accidentally licking each other.

On my third or fourth day there, they bring in a homeless boy who has, like many patients, been picked up from the streets. He has a swastika carved into his forehead because voices told him to do it. I am extremely scared of him, so I force myself to make conversation. He asks what I'm listening to on my Walkman and, ashamed, I say, "George Michael." "I like George Michael," he says, furious at me for making it seem shameful. Never use pop culture as delineator with someone who hears voices. You don't know what they hear between the melodies. On my last day, I leave him my Walkman and all my music. I wonder if it's easier to navigate a stay in a psychiatric hospital now iPods exist, or if it impedes progress.

There is a lovely middle-aged man, a straitlaced dad with small children, calm and sweet and I cannot for the life of me work out what's wrong with him, so even is his voice and energy. It turns out that he broke his leg and arm climbing a generator pole. He waited until he healed and then did it again. "Why did you do it again?" he is asked in group therapy. "Why that pole?"

He looks at the therapist like she's mad. "Because that's the pole that leads to heaven."

The grounds are very beautiful at the Priory. Somewhat Edward Gorey, a little Aubrey Beardsley. One expects to see peacocks, and I imagine there must be patients who, in fact, do see peacocks. It is a place for a gothic love affair. A place to hide from the world. It isn't until I leave that place that I go out and find love for the first time. That could be because I got well (I doubt it) or because the grounds have, by osmosis, worked their way into me. This is love: beautiful, secret, overgrown, last chance.

A nurse from the juvenile ward comes up to me in the cafeteria one day. "Emma?" I blink. It takes a moment to recognize her as a friend of a friend. We all used to go dancing. Thankfully, I am too tired and too medicated to feel any embarrassment, even when she asks, "So . . . how have you been?"

I look at her a moment. "Not so good."

She lets it go and moves on with her rounds.

For some reason, I care deeply about what I wear in the hospital. I'm still thin enough to wear curious things.

Have you ever eaten something appalling for breakfast, something really bad for you, a chocolate cake, and just thought, "Fuck it, this is bad, I'd better keep going? Christ, this is making me feel horrible, I'd better have more?"

And then have you ever left the last bite, less than the last bite, a morsel, a crumb even, and said to yourself, "There, I didn't finish it. That didn't really happen. You don't process the calories unless it's the final crumby morsel. Everyone knows that. So, we're cool, right?"

And you walk away whistling and try to think of worse things you might leave a crumb of, come lunchtime. If that all sounds bulimic, it is. The mind-set is: I've started on a path I'd prefer not to be on and I'm ashamed so I'd better just keep going. Somewhere along the line it becomes a perfectly routine and reasonable thing to be doing of an afternoon. All self-inflicted pain is excess consumption— heroin, crack, sex, food—even anorexia is its own path you can't turn back from, more air, more nothing, space filled, to bursting, with space. Anorexia didn't suit me, because I couldn't make it work fast enough. The medium is the message, and my medium was cutting and bulimia.

Chicken and egg: Which comes first, looking at yourself with burst blood vessels on your eyes and vomit in your hair and having to cut yourself because you're so ugly? Or eating everything in the cupboard to try to hold down how ugly the cutting has made you? It is madness. And if you don't know who you are, or if your real self has drifted away from you with the undertow, madness at least gives you an identity.

It's the same with self-loathing. You're probably just normal and normal-looking but that's not a real identity, not the way ugliness is. Normality, just accepting that you're probably normal-looking, lacks the force field of self-disgust.

If you don't know who you are, madness gives you something to believe in, and whilst I am locked away at the Priory, melting into mine, GH makes the public eye with his. On our group TV, there's a flicker of him being interviewed about his first big film. He seems drunk. "What," I say to my anorexic pal, "a fool."

She snorts. "I wouldn't kick him out of bed." She doesn't have the strength to kick.

I also snuck in a disposable camera.

This turns out to be not smart, as patients begin to act out. One woman shows up to see me with burns on her cheeks where she's set fire to herself with a lighter. I put my camera away. I use up the film taking photos of myself in my bed, proto-MySpace pictures, cheeks sucked in, lips pouting. I've noticed it since in Lindsay Lohan's and Britney Spears's self-portraits: they always suck in their cheeks and pout no matter the circumstances, seemingly unaware that it's the scars, not the cheekbones, that catch the light in their Twitter posts.

After a week, I'm still fuzzy, but boredom is starting to creep in around the edges. In art therapy I paint a picture of young Rod Stewart and title it *Rod the Mod!* I cannot tell you what possessed me. He means nothing to me, but it is a good likeness. The art teacher makes a big fuss and says it's very revealing. I feel sorry for her. The middle-aged dad draws the telegraph pole he cannot stop climbing. It means everything to him. She moves past it quickly.

The pills they have me on leave me catatonic for much of the day. It feels like I'm moving in mud. Mum says my eyes are rolling back in my head. "Maybe," I agree, and think about how much I like circles, and Kandinsky, and then visiting hour is used up and she leaves. Because I'm a suicide case, after lights-out, they check on me every five minutes. A few days before I am let out altogether, my mum is allowed to take me into London for a Saturday visit. We go to the movies, *Erin Brockovich*, for which Julia Roberts wins an Oscar whilst forgetting to thank Erin Brockovich herself. Can it be true that I ride the tube back to the hospital alone? I know that I look people in the eye until they have to look away. There is an element of being so frightened of myself that I'm gratified to find I frighten the public at large. I am allowed out after two weeks, diagnosed as a rapid cycle manic-depressive, which is to say, instead of six months in bed then six months raving, my mood changes wildly within an hour.

I don't think the Priory was especially helpful, beyond giving me a forced vacation from life and debts it would take many years to pay off.

GROVELANDS PRIORY HOSPITAL

INITIAL TESTS & ASSESSMENTS £300.00
(Charged once on an admission in addition to bed fee)

DAILY BED FEE—Standard £325.00

DAILY BED FEE—High Dependency £355.00

DAILY CONSULTANT FEE £45.00
(A daily fee charged by your consultant for retaining clinical responsibility for your care. Although the consultant is responsible for your care throughout your stay, they may not see you every day.)

The daily bed fee covers accommodation (single room with bathroom), basic nursing care, duty psychiatrist and junior doctor cover, medication, treatment programme, and all meals.

A deposit of £3000.00 is required on admission, followed by £3000.00 weekly thereafter for the duration of the admission (please see "Financial Requirements for Self-funding Admissions").

ADDITIONAL CLINICAL CHARGES
(Billed where appropriate)
Initial Consultant's Fee   Charged per consultant
Special Nursing   £26.00
(Charged per hour in addition to the Standard Daily Bed Fee)
ECG   £96.00 each

ECT	£211.00 each
Physiotherapy	Charged per session
Ambulance/Transport	Charged per journey
Nurse Escort	£19 per hour
X-rays & Scans	Charged per procedure
Family Therapy	£85.00 per session
Discharge Medication	£10 per day

ADDITIONAL PERSONAL EXPENSES

Newspapers/Magazines etc.	Charged per item
Telephone calls	24p per unit
Guest Meals (tickets available on Reception)	
Main Meal	£7.50 each
Snack	£3.50 each

THERAPEUTIC LEAVE	DISCHARGE
1st and 2nd night—Charged full daily fee Before 2pm	No Charge
3rd night away—Charged half daily fee 2pm–6pm	Charged half full daily fee
Subsequent nights—no charge After 6pm	Charged full daily fee

The Admissions Secretary or Accounts staff will be happy to advise on all accounts of these fees.

My first night back home, Dad is doodling in felt-tip pen on pages of the *National Enquirer*. He looks up from his work and says, "I would like to stay home all day and draw mustaches on pictures of Britney Spears." Spears is still young and desirable, not yet Blanche DuBois in Daisy Dukes.

I hope his mustachioing her so close to my exit from the psych ward did not doom Britney, by ink, to the same fate.

There is a Priory doctor I am compelled to see as an out-patient. I don't remember much about him, but I have all his bills. I have his follow-up letters where he doesn't know my name or my mum's name but he sure is trying to get my money. I imagine it as a chapter in a Helen Gurley Brown book: "*A modern girl pays for her own psychiatric treatment.*"

Almost immediately, I want to get back to my apartment—even in my state I am enough of a New Yorker to know that it's a steal I oughtn't let go. I want to get back to Manhattan. And I want to get back to Dr. R. I call him from my parents'. We speak for half an hour, long enough for him to decide he doesn't like the drug the Priory put me on. Depakote, too 1950s—though that seems fitting to me, throwback girl that I am. (Maybe I'm on the same drug as Bettie Page! I think. I'm still to some extent excited by my madness.) Later I will find out that Dr. R is an exception-ally gifted psychopharmacologist, which is why his initial miscalculation hurt him. He gets it right next time. For now it's just his voice on the phone that helps stabilize my mood.

MAY 16, 2008

Nine years ago, Dr. R saved my life. Because of him, my parents got their daughter back. We are forever indebted, and eternally grateful for the gift of his presence in our lives. Over the years, I teased him about being a terminal optimist. Thank goodness he was one; I rode on the coattails of his faith and enthusiasm for a long time.

I will carry Dr. R with me always. I will strive to emulate his kindness and poise, especially around those who are sick and suffering, as I was when I had the good fortune to have landed under his care.

This loss is too large to describe.

ANNA (NEW YORK, NY)

CHAPTER 7

THERE'S A SET OF PHOTOS of me in my bra and panties and knee-high socks, bleeding all over the place. They were taken by an unnamed photographer, a fashion god, the week before the suicide attempt.

"Maybe I should hang on to these," says Dr. R when I show him.

"No."

I stretch out my hand. I walk over to him, hover above his seat.

"I look fat."

He doesn't sigh or gasp. He makes some notes.

"You know you're not fat."

"I know that. I said that I *look* fat."

I take them from his hand, put them away, and snap: "What's the point of being one way, if you appear, in posterity, to be another?"

"Whether or not you look bigger than you are in a photo

is not what defines you. It would define some women. Shallow, disturbed women. Not you."

No matter how many times I stood before him saying, "I am shallow. I am disturbed," he'd never repeat it back to me. In a romantic relationship, you can make the person say that. I always got my boyfriends to say it back to me.

If you piss behind a lamppost when you're twenty, that's carefree and eccentric and bold. If you piss behind a lamppost when you're thirty-eight, that's just disgusting. Isn't it? If you're a man making eyes at girls at twenty, that's raffish. If you're doing it at thirty-eight, it's foul. People don't know. We don't know ourselves so we tell ourselves what we really know is other people.

We could say the depth of pain we feel for the lovers who've left us is because we knew them so well.

I have intense pain for Dr. R and longing and actually a genuine connection. But I didn't know him at all. And in that sense, he is a safety zone. The safest and also most challenging loss I can conjure. I mean, who is it I'm longing for? I know a little bit from our sessions and a little bit from his obituary.

He loved: Barbara (obituary).
He loved: Sam and Andy (obituary).
He loved: *The West Wing* (our sessions).
He loved: windsurfing (obituary).
He taught at: Columbia (Barbara told me).
He specialized in: cocaine psychosis (his books on Amazon).

He summered in: the Hamptons (our sessions).

He loved: musicals (our sessions).

I don't know where he died. I don't know how he died. I need to know.

I do know that Dr. R has been in my life for over eight years because I am growing sad wondering what he would make of Barack Obama. And then silly things. When someone dies too young you think of all the things he will miss, his children growing up, his twilight years with his wife, but you also say, "I cannot believe he missed Tina Fey's impersonation of Sarah Palin." You stretch heavenward for his wisdom (regardless of whether you believe in heaven, it's where you stretch, much as suicides who jump off bridges die with dislocated arms, instinctively trying to grab back on) and in the same breath can't stand that he missed out on Tina Fey's impression of a woman he didn't live to see.

CHAPTER 8

———————

IT'S JUST OVER SIX MONTHS since I got out of the hospital and I want to watch election coverage with my friends around me, but my house is too filthy to allow anyone in, so I rent a hotel room. I am still living in disarray; I am still spending money wildly (easier to rent a hotel suite than to tidy up); I still cannot understand why anyone thinks my cutting is problematic. Oh! Here's something funny! When I got back from hospital, Bad Boyfriend and my English Flatmate had become a couple. So I'm in contact with neither. But I am not too upset, because there's a boy—Mike—whose affection I am determined to hunt down and kill. It used to be material objects I felt I needed to be happy. At eleven, I knew "things would be better if only I had a floor-length floral skirt in autumn colors." Grandma knuckled down and made the skirt of my imagination for me. I put it on. And then I cried, because things weren't any better.

I have tried to find happiness through hair color. Election 2000, I have hair that is supposed to be blond but has turned out an ash-y orange. SB says it is the exact same shade as the toupee worn by a *Sopranos* villain called Ralph Cifaretto, who beat a teenage mistress to death. "That isn't how I want to look," I explain to my mother in our daily call.

"Oh!" she says, "but his hair's nice!"

So, I look like Ralph Cifaretto, Florida is in the balance, and I'm determined that Mike, being corn-fed and Mid-western, would make me feel stable if I had him. If I had someone like him, it would prove that I'm stable, and then I wouldn't have to do the work to get there. Mike is just a nice boy from Ohio. Ohio Mike. When I am sent to inter-view Brad Pitt for the cover of *Esquire*, the first words out of my mouth when he walks into the room are: "*Oh*. You aren't as good-looking as Ohio Mike."

"Who's Ohio Mike?" asks Pitt, good-naturedly, for he is nothing if not good-natured.

I have long sleeves with special holes so I can hook them over my thumbs, not a smidge of skin viewable, so covered is it in cuts.

"This guy I like, who's better-looking than you."

There are two stories I remember (intertwined by the hy-permania), one story of love and one of art, and both of a kind of revolution that I like very much. I dwell on the tale of Che Guevara picking up Aleida, who would become his wife, by telling her he was off to overthrow the Bolivian government and did she want to come with him?

The other I obsess over is Bob Dylan seeing the violinist Scarlet Rivera walking along the road with her violin case and spontaneously asking her to come to the studio with him. *Desire* comes out of it the year I am born. Violins at a

revolution. Icons trying to get their wives to stay, others se-
ducing them for the first time. Sometimes Bob Dylan is the
one who, in my head, ends up dead and posed, Christ-like,
at the hands of the CIA. Che, meanwhile, briefly converts
to Christianity and writes an ill-received screenplay.

Maybe it's because I'm manic, but I can conjure people.
A week after nonstop listening to *Desire*, I see Bob Dylan on
the streets of downtown New York.

To my Soho Grand election suite, SB and I have corralled:
Ohio Mike, his friends Ohio Bob and Ohio Joe. They are
enormous men, shaped like beer cans with legs. They work
with their hands and own their own power tools. I haven't
known men like them. I'm used to London boys with their
skinny ties and bodies. Or pear-shaped Jewish men from the
family tree. They haven't known girls like me. SB can tell
that things are not going to work out well in this election
and she is in the corner, reading Philip Roth.

None of these boys needs or wants his soul to be fought
for. God, I've got so much fight in me and no one to throw
it at (a game of dodgeball, because at least if I could save
someone through love, I would be dodging myself).

To that end, I am an appalling show-off.

"If Bush gets in I'm chucking my shoes out the window,"
I announce, because not enough people are looking at me.

The result is indecisive because of Florida, so I throw one
shoe out the window. I immediately regret it, as I do with
so many of my manic decisions. TiVo hasn't been invented
and yet my life is already littered with TiVo moments: just
let me rewind that. Just let me skip that part. That didn't
happen!

I can see it, my high-top Nike in the snow beyond someone's fence, so near and yet so far. I walk home in my one
sneaker, the snow the same gray mush as a hung parliament.
On the corner of Bleecker and Sixth Avenue I see Susan Sarandon zooming toward me on a scooter. I have never met
her, but she's part of my father's nonsense world. If you eat
one of my dad's French fries he snaps, "Oh! I was saving
that for Susan Sarandon's séance!" On his website, jeffrey
friedchicken.com, you can find a partial inventory of other
things being saved for the big day (a copy of the *Independent*,
a Twinkie, Ron Howard).

I look at Susan Sarandon, so gracefully balanced on her
scooter and in her life. I am constantly looking for ways to
cede control of my worries to someone, anyone, and she's
in front of me, so I stop her and, without introducing myself, ask: "Susan? How the hell are we going to get through
four years of George Bush?"

It's 2000, so I don't even know the half of it. She brakes
her scooter and fixes me.

"Well, we got through the first one. We'll get through
the second."

She has that same rhythm of calm as Dr. R.

Snow-scooter Susan sees me through until my next
session.

CHAPTER 9

I'M CURLED UP IN the leather chair like a cat, and Dr. R's leaned into his leather chair like a far classier cat. I smile at him. He smiles back and writes something on his yellow notepad.

"What are you writing?"

"Just making notes."

"About me?"

He rolls his eyes. "Yes, about you."

"Are you drawing me?"

"Sort of."

I decide that if Dr. R were in a boy band, he'd be the cheeky one.

"If you were in a boy band, you'd be the cheeky one."

"Huh?"

"Yeah, they all have a different personality type. Like: the cheeky one, the innocent one, the tough one!"

I think.

"They could do a boy band of psychiatric disorders. . . . The bipolar one, the body dysmorphic one . . ."

"Right, the obsessive-compulsive one."

"And if it were a spin-off series, right, like *The Colbys* was from *Dynasty* . . ."

"What's that?"

"Yeah, *Dynasty* had this spin-off *The Colbys*. Anyway, then they could have a spin-off with unclassifiable phobias, like the one with a fear of dancing."

"That's chorophobia."

"OK, the one with a fear of himself."

"That's called autophobia."

"Wow. There's a name for everybody."

"Pretty much."

I sniff, as if I'm not sure what to ask next, though I'm exactly sure.

"So . . . what am I?"

"It's not always helpful to classify."

He writes something down.

"Seriously. What am I?"

He smiles again.

"You're Emma."

This would be a good time to say, I have tried several psychiatrists and therapists, from age eight on. It's in our blood as Jews; it's in our blood as intellectuals; as bourgeois, maybe; *maybe* it's in our blood because we are psychiatrically unwell.

INVENTORY: *Unsuccessful therapists I have had before finding Dr. R*

1 × *Hungarian counselor (unfortunate memories of Cloris Leachman in* Young Frankenstein*)*

*1 × Well-coiffed blonde who had home office next to house we
couldn't afford to buy (unfortunate memories of Catherine
Deneuve in* Belle de Jour: *bored housewife moonlights as
shrink instead of hooker. Note to self: good idea for film)*

*1 × Well-intentioned Jewess (unfortunate memories of the
great-aunts I had to write thank-you letters to when they sent
me things that itched. Pavlov's Dog says: I itched throughout
her sessions)*

Why would an eight-year-old need a therapist? Well, anyone who can have a therapist should have one. That's what I
remember my mother saying. Also. I was mad. No. I was in
trouble. I was under threat of expulsion.

As I write it down, it is no small thing—that the beginning of this path to "wellness" was under duress, that I was
sent there as a villain. I was also sent there wrongly accused.
This is the truth. I didn't do it. I wanted to. And then I got
scared. Ella did it. Her mother blamed me. I told Ella we
should send Lucy a sex note and pretend it was from a boy
in the year above. It was literally "Meet me in the library
after school for more sex." I wrote the note, then chickened
out. Ella took it out of my school bag and placed it in Lucy's
desk. The headmistress had the handwriting analyzed. I
swear to G-d, she did everything but call in MI5.

Did they know that I didn't do it, I recently asked my
parents? "Well, no." Why had I never spoken up before?
Well, these things just start to matter less, is that it? Or is it
that we take the roles we are handed because it is a relief, no
matter how unflattering, to have a role? Even in the unfair-
ness, was there a gratitude at not having to figure myself

out because they had decided for me? And because they had done that, I was sent to my first shrink to figure myself out. Which never happened. Not at that age. I just relished the chocolate brownie my mum bought me on the way to the sessions.

I told my classmates I was going to Hebrew lessons, which was a weird invention given that my sister and I were the only Jews at school. How to make me seem like even more of an outsider. But I kept eating that brownie, looking at the therapist's built-up shoes. People decided I was getting better, and I was even invited to a party. My mum took me to get a special outfit, preparing for this party to which a child had been forced to invite me because my mother had complained that invitations ought not be handed out in class if the whole class was not invited. Preparing me for something to which I was not welcome and had no place.

What was funny was the mothers who openly disliked me. They knew, because they were adults, that something was off with me, something that would never fall into place. Girls would corner me in the bathroom to tell me: "*My* mother says *your* family are common."

Lucy, she of the note, said, "Don't you feel bad for killing Christ?" and I said, "No, I feel good," and then she called me a nigger. Lucy was Greek. It took until I was twenty-seven, on a 6 train up to Dr. R's, to think to myself, Hey, hang on. On the ethnic scale, if Nubian is out here and Swede is over there, surely Jew and Greek fall in the same place?

"Dr. R? Don't you think, on the ethnic scale, that Jew and Greek fall in the same place?"

"It sounds right. On the contributions to mankind scale too."

I take a piece of his paper and painstakingly draw him the ethnic scale.

"Does it matter?" he asks.

"Yes."

"Why?"

"Because it wasn't fair."

He raises his eyebrows. Writes something down.

"Have you ever known life to be fair?"

"No."

"It would be a funny time to start."

"Yeah."

"Probably better to just run with the good things."

I look at the diagram I drew. "Jews win."

"How do you figure that?"

"Duh!" I hand him the piece of paper. "We invented psychiatry."

I smile.

"And then we wrote songs about it."

I sing: "Officer Krupke, you're really a square / This boy don't need a judge, he needs an analyst's care . . ."

Dr. R, beaming, sings, really badly: "It's just his neurosis that oughta be curbed / he's psychologically disturbed!"

We had a lot of fun in our sessions. Our sessions were often the most cheerful I was in a week. Not manic, like when I listen to "Pata Pata" by Miriam Makeba fourteen times in a row. Just properly happy. Other patients remember him as a natty dresser, but to me Dr. R dressed awkwardly, like my dad, who wears shorts and black leather lawyer shoes at beach resorts.

"You know how all Jewish men are kind of gay?" I ask Dr. R not long after we meet.

"Yes!" he says, quite earnestly, swiveling in his chair.

Encouraged, I add, "Like how they all love musicals?"

"I love musicals!"

"Yeah, my dad does . . ."

"Which one's his favorite?"

"Um, *The Music Man?*"

"I *love The Music Man!*"

From the start, Dr. R feels like family, but in a good way. Like a family member you'd never have to write a thank-you letter to because he'd never send you something that itched.

One afternoon, I come to his office quite agitated.

"You know the band Coldplay?"

He shakes his head.

"Yes you do."

He shrugs. "OK. Fine. You're seeing one of them?"

"Hell NO! Jesus, Dr. R! Why do you assume that?"

"Track record."

"OK. Right. Coldplay. They're a band and they're really popular and the singer is called Chris Martin and I keep seeing him in my neighborhood running errands and wearing a ridiculous hat."

"So?"

"It's sort of a felt jester's hat made out of wool. Why is Chris Martin wearing that hat? What does it mean?"

He puts his hands out in front of him like a Borscht Belt comic trying to get the audience to settle down. "I don't think it means anything, Emma."

"It means something."

He distracts me away from distraction.

"I'm more concerned about the cutting."

"Really?" I say this like, "How eccentric of you."

He raises his eyebrows at the page. I catch from him in occasional split seconds an inner sigh of, She's a cuckoo clock! It makes me trust him more.

When people say, "How are you?" he's the only one to whom I can truly answer, "Dude! I am not OK."

He never says, "I am not your dude."

CHAPTER 10

_____

I MEET GLORIA STEINEM after my friend the poet and activist Sarah Jones tells her about a novel I wrote, an opus of self-mutilation. Gloria Steinem, whom I have admired from so far for so long, listens as I describe the book, then asks if I was sexually abused. Did I say we're on an escalator? After a screening of _The Manchurian Candidate?_ The remake with Meryl Streep? And that I'm holding a half-empty bucket of popcorn? I swivel my head up to Steinem from the moving step below.

"No. I wasn't sexually abused."

She says, "Are you sure?"

I say that I'm sure, and offer her some popcorn.

The Tiffany lamp seems exceptionally bright in East 94th Street that session.

"Dr. R. Gloria Steinem told me most cutters were sexually abused."

"A significant portion," he says, turning down the lamp, knowing by now which squint refers to which circumstantial discomfort.

"Right, so a majority of cutters were sexually abused. It's just that: I wasn't."

"OK."

"So, like, I sounded really super-defensive and evasive with one of my great heroines. On a moving staircase."

This turns out to be a double session, something we rarely do. And it's funny we take up so much time, because he's unusually silent. I hear myself talking and think, Stop talking now, let him say something now. But I don't.

"I wasn't sexually abused as a kid. I was, I think, like almost every woman I know, sexually weirded-out as a kid."

He nods. "Anything specific?"

Of course, of course something specific. Something with a specific landscape and even a specific scent. I put my head on my knees, and then sit up again.

"I was working for the *Sunday Times*, writing about music. I was sixteen. I'd never had sex. I met this woman at a Breeders show I was reviewing." I look up. "They're a great, great band." I say this as if it somehow qualifies what's coming next. "And this woman was from San Francisco and we talked the whole show and late into the night—she was forty and really beautiful and there alone—and she said, 'Come stay with me in California.'"

She was tiny, with very white skin and a platinum bob, as if Louise Brooks's hairdo got ruined in the wash.

"She was sort of mystical, how she looked, how she talked, that she was there at all, in this sea of moshing teenagers. She made me think of one of the goddesses on my oracle cards. Wait. I have that the wrong way. She gave me my first pack of goddess cards. I didn't know, until after I left her, what she reminded me of. Anyway. You know I've always loved being around older women . . ."

"I know."

"And she was in a fucking band!"

Not a successful band, they hadn't been signed yet, and at forty, it was probably unlikely. But they gigged regularly in San Francisco, had a following there.

"So I went to stay with her for a week, going there with, honestly, with this huge crush. I'd never been with a woman, but I really, really wanted to be with her. She gave off absolutely no vibes that she was that way inclined, by the way. I was just fixated on her, the way I've been fixated on a dress or a book or a lipstick."

He's making a ballpoint dash here and a ballpoint dash there, and he looks up for half a moment and simply smiles when I say:

"She didn't mention she had a husband.

"I'd just landed, and there she is at the airport, waiting for me, and she takes me for lunch at a pier-side restaurant. She waves in the middle distance as this beautiful boy walks towards us. But he doesn't stop when he sees her: he keeps walking, right to the edge, then he dives into the water. And as all the restaurant patrons gape, he climbs out of the water, shakes himself like a dog, and sits down with us.

"Her husband was much younger than her. He was in his twenties, maybe his early twenties, it's hard to judge other people's ages when you're sixteen. Everybody's just *older*. Everybody is nefarious and wants you and has ulterior motives and everybody is playing at Dangerous Liaisons. You know?"

Tick. Dr. R goes: tick, on his notepad.

"So her husband was completely surly and rude. He barely acknowledged me when she introduced us and it took me the lunch to understand that they were married. They argued all through dessert and they never stopped. My heart was pounding and I thought, I'm sixteen, where am I, what have I done?

"We got to their apartment and I realized they had to walk past my daybed to get in and out of their room. She and I would spend our days on the beach—she'd photograph me in my bikini. I pretended I was Bettie Page and she was Bunny Yeager, you know, the female photographer who made Bettie a star. She'd take all these pictures of me and I loved posing for her. I had all this tits and ass that felt exciting in a strange land. Back home in England, the tits and ass just felt like bad omens.

"At night I'd hear them argue, screaming fights, and I'd hide under the blankets, like a kid and her parents.

"He got into my bed one night, said he needed to talk. That they couldn't stop fighting and he didn't know what to do. I was flattered. I told him that I knew she loved him and they'd sort it out.

"What did I know? I'd never had a boyfriend. My platinum-bobbed beauty started to be too busy during the afternoons to hang out with me—she had a new shift in a bar. So she assigned him to keep me entertained. We went to see *Two-Lane Blacktop* at a revival cinema. The film was confused, largely silent, and bubbling with sexual curiosity, just like me.

"He took me on a motorbike ride across the Golden Gate Bridge. I was shaking so hard the motorbike was starting to swerve and he was saying 'Goddamnit, Emma! You're shaking like a fucking leaf! You're making the bike swerve. We're gonna have an accident!'

"We nearly did, several times. By the time he let me off, I was drained of all color, all feeling. It was evening, and he said I needed a shot.

"Then we were watching her band play. She had this great girl playing bass. Then we were at a bar. No. Then we were at a bar, then we were watching her band play. He had been feeding me Jägermeister shots. I couldn't stand up, and her band was done, and she wanted to stay out and party. I was spoiling it.

"So he told her he'd walk me home. They kissed for a really long time before we left.

"We were in an alleyway when he said that he had seen the photographs she'd been taking of me in my bikini, on the beach.

"And then he kissed me.

"And I kissed him back."

I wait for Dr. R to write that down. He doesn't.

"Then I stopped kissing him back. But he kept going. He moved me forward until we were leaning against a church and I could see a stained-glass window. No light was re-fracting through it, because it was night. He pulled down my pants. Because it was from behind, and because I had never had sex, I didn't even know if it was normal sex or if that meant it was anal sex."

Dr. R still isn't writing.

"It didn't hurt much. I wasn't there. He said he couldn't help it. He said it was because of my body."

I look at my feet. I have on red sneakers I don't ever re-member buying.

"If it didn't hurt much and I wasn't there, what was it? What am I upset about? Why did it leave me feeling marked?"

He says nothing.

"Afterwards, on the street, we ran into her bassist. She sensed something weird and asked if I wanted to go hang out at her place and he let me go off with her. So I went to her loft, with all these hippie musicians hanging out, and she laid me down on the sofa and I told her, I wasn't crying or anything, I just said, really matter-of-factly, 'I think I've just had sex.'

"It wasn't the thing of it that upset me so much as the name of it. I passed out cold on the sofa, and when I woke up, she said, 'I called the . . .'"

I don't like this part. I really, really don't like this part, for so many reasons. I start to cry.

"She said, 'I called the rape hotline.'

"I didn't ask her to do that."

Dr. R finally looks up. "You were unconscious, how could you?"

I shrug.

"When he pulled down your pants, you asked him to stop?"

"Yes."

"Because?"

"Because I didn't want to have sex."

"He didn't stop."

"No. I wanted him, I guess. But not like that. I'd never

even made out with a boy. But mainly, I was devastated because I lost her, my platinum blonde. I wrote, like, these love letters and she never replied. What I heard through the bassist was, he had told his wife I hit on him and he made a mistake."

I remember, on the plane, I was too sore to sit down.

I remember too, that before I lost consciousness on the bassist's sofa, one of her roommates was playing Leonard Cohen, splicing together different lyrics of Cohen admiring the female nude. My dad and I had seen him play the year before at the Royal Albert Hall. And now Leonard Cohen was there in the aftermath I couldn't tell my dad about. Links and ribbons, people knowing things without knowing. I'll love Leonard for the rest of my life. My lids heavy from the Jägermeister, a searing discomfort in my vagina, the last voice you hear . . .

"So, anyway," I tell Dr. R, "I don't like standing-up sex." I'm ready to change the subject now.

"It's funny that you associate certain positions with certain lovers when you get old enough. There's 'the one who always wanted me to sit on his face.' 'The one who always wanted me on top, facing away so he could see my ass.' Bianca says it's called 'Reverse Cowgirl.'"

Dr. R blushes. I don't like making him blush so I'm trying to joke it all away now, inventing sexual positions to make him laugh: "Extravagant Car Phone." "Rheumatic Kitten."

He interrupts me. "It doesn't matter what you call it, it was a transgression. If you'd been having sex for ten years, it would be rough sex. But it was the first."

"Yep."

The truth is: I lost my virginity. In an unpleasant manner. But I lost her too, and that felt worse. She had taken me to her favorite apothecary and I'd bought this moisturizer she used because it smelled of her. I took it home with me to London. I'd made myself a promise: I'll use this every day, and when the bottle runs out, that's the moment I'll be over what happened in San Francisco. But I could never bring myself to use it. It's still under the sink in my childhood bathroom at my parents' house. I can't imagine it smells any good; I'm too scared to open it. But, sometimes, when I go home, I look at it, and I can see that the moisturizer has separated from the oil. Something's risen to the top.

"You could take that as a happy allegory."

"No. Because I look at it and realize something in it is dead, that it must be made of whale fat."

"It's from San Francisco. The moisturizer was probably vegan."

"OK," I say. "OK, you win. Optimist."

Time's up.

CHAPTER 11

————————

DR. R AND I keep plowing from the last session. I tell him about my first love, a man for whom I was most emphatically not his first love or, indeed, his love at all. It was a few months after San Francisco. He was in a rock band. I was a teenage music journalist. He sent me postcards, sometimes, not often, from tour. He sent me a couple of books. *Memoirs of a Revolutionary* by Victor Serge arrived, inscribed with elaborate indifference.

When I gave in to him he sighed and said, "We're similar, Em. We'll always be the least attractive people in the room." A sort of postcoital contempt. After we'd make love, he'd tell me the reasons I wasn't pretty and how he was special for wanting me. That's when the cutting kicked off.

"I used to cut myself when I knew I was going to run into him, so I couldn't take my clothes off. So I wouldn't lose my heart to him. Though, of course, I already had."

Dr. R looks very, very sad. "Did that work?"

"No. I wanted him so much, I'd go home with him anyway. And he didn't see the cuts. He never noticed. If he did he didn't say anything. He just fucked me anyway." I start to cry, amazed that the man who I thought had vanished ten years earlier, like Brigadoon, can still have this effect. I don't like saying "fuck" in front of Dr. R. I hate it. I feel like I sully this room.

Though, really, what am I sullying? I don't know what stories came before or which will be here with the patient after me. Suddenly I want to cover my mouth, afraid of breathing psychological germs, and get out of there, leaving my lovelorn teenage self in London, on her knees, before a man who cannot stand her.

CHAPTER 12

─────────

I met Dr. R at a particularly hard time in my life. It was by chance that I was referred to him on my birthday nine years ago.

When I called to make the appointment he said he had a cancellation. He said how about January 19. I said it was not good, it was my forty-ninth birthday; who goes to the doctor on their birthday, and he responded, "Why not, it's as good a day as ever." He was wise that way.

In retrospect, I now think of my first visit with Dr. R as the best birthday present I have ever been given.

I did not know that Dr. R was ill. I saw him several months ago. He was his usual upbeat, caring, focused, insightful self. He never lost a step in his stride. I realize now how brave he was that day. I will—forever—remember him as my hero.

M (NEW YORK, NY)

"I know you're getting better because of how you coped with nine-eleven. Other patients didn't do so well."

I shrug. "Mental people don't like apocalypse."

He looks me dead on. "Many of my patients were triggered by it. Not you."

As the day had unfolded, even my toughest friends had become hysterical. They said there were still planes in the sky. They said we were about to have bombs dropped from above. We all gathered at SB's, and I persuaded the group that we had to go to the hospital and give blood. So that's where we went. But there was no one to give blood to because nobody was alive.

"I realize," I tell Dr. R, "that I'm really, really bad at navigating life's pointless daily pain. And that I'm better at handling catastrophe."

Living so close to St. Vincent's hospital, I follow the outsider art that springs up on the walls of the building in the form of "Missing" posters. You see the families who could afford to laminate them, with five different phone numbers and contacts. And the barely legible ones that look like they were copied at the deli. When the rains wash away the badly printed ones in Spanish, I do sit down on the sidewalk and weep. I sit with them every day because there is nothing I can do but say "I'm sorry" and "See, you were loved. So much." In life, there would have been times, maybe many times, that those people in the posters had felt misunderstood and alone. And now the lonely ache is someone else's, forever.

It's around this time that I start seeing a writer who is almost as famous for his tumultuous private life as he is his award-winning work. I watch Dr. R as I tell him the news.

Other people have been impressed. They cannot help it. Dr.
R has talked about him before, what a fan he is. I am eager to
watch him cover his excitement. Even my own mum couldn't
hide how tickled she was that he is interested in me. When I
tell Dr. R, he doesn't look excited at all. He looks crestfallen.

"I am concerned. I am very concerned about a relapse if
you keep seeing him."

And indeed the writer has me in knots for a year, and a
hold that extends for many, many years. He's so present in
our sessions, I reckon he should split the check.

When Dr. R dies, this writer is one of the first people I
want to tell. Because he was there for so many of our sessions. Because we battled over him.

It's gotten to the point where, as soon as I mention him,
Dr. R puts his head in his hands. I like very much when he
puts his head in his hands because it means he noticed me, he
really noticed me. This is the essence of my descent into cutting: you are caught between a terrible secret and a terrible
secret that once revealed means people are looking, people
are listening. Your pain can no longer be ignored or misread.

Dr. R takes a breath and sits up. "I don't want you to see
him again."

"But I *cannot* stop thinking about him."

"Write about it."

"How?"

"Write a screenplay."

For two weeks, I am that person in a café with a laptop.
And after two weeks I have a screenplay. And because a writer
threw me out of a speeding car and broke my heart, Dr. R
told me to write a script and I do and it gets me signed by

William Morris and then I have a new accidental career that only really starts to blossom after Dr. R is too sick to know.

He knew I signed with William Morris and moved out to L.A. That's as far as he got.

Your child should not die before you. Your shrink should not die before you. When I tried to kill myself, my mum went uptown to see her old shrink, her old therapist from when she was my age. Some people look into the future and imagine themselves at their daughter's wedding. I always had this romantic dream: that when my daughter had a breakdown, I'd go uptown to see Dr. R.

INVENTORY: *Places to cut yourself*

Thigh

Bikini line

Neck

Ankles

Upper arms

Forearms

New York

Los Angeles

London

Wellington

(Sunset Strip hotel room special)

The Chateau Marmont

The Standard

The Mondrian

There is a very long break in cutting after that stay at the Mondrian. I'm there, courtesy of Sony Music, interviewing the very gifted, very troubled soul singer Macy Gray for the *Telegraph*. In talking to her over several days, I have the strong sense, as she talks to the wall, as she mumbles into her hands, that she is never coming back to land. This throws me. This is the first time I am conscious of being the sane one in the conversation.

_____

CHAPTER 13

INVENTORY: *Men I have masturbated about*

Martin Sheen in the opening scene of Apocalypse Now, *where he's drunk and cutting himself with broken glass*

Cat Stevens, inside jacket of Teaser and the Firecat

Bob Dylan, wearing a waistcoat and clown makeup, in video of the 1975 Rolling Thunder Revue *tour*

So that's an addict. Addict turned fundamentalist. Mentalist.

Also: Topol, in Fiddler on the Roof, *when he thrusts his chest and bellows "YA DA DA DA DA DA!" But I don't know what he is except for just plain strange*

To summarize: Are you an alcoholic/extremist/narcissist and/or lusty-voiced shtetl dweller?

I love you.

Lay readers would surely, like Dr. R before them, say that men, and the pursuit of them, are strongly intertwined with my mental health. I would say, in my defensive defense, that the problem with being a serial monogamist is, there isn't anybody random or unimportant: everybody you sleep with really means something, which is to say each of them is on your public record.

At some point I wake up thinking, Fuck this! I don't want another man in my bed ever again. What I really want is a cat.

After a month of waking with this thought every single day, I persuade Dr. R to let me adopt a shelter cat. This is a big deal. I'm allowed to look after something other than me. Odd though it may sound, it's the biggest step I'd ever taken towards my mental health. It takes me out of the realm of men, makes me stay healthy, makes me a modicum less selfish, loads more responsible. Of course, I get a boy cat.

Perry's owner was killed on 9/11. When we meet, he is in a cage, at a pet store, having been passed on from a shelter when nobody claimed him. Now, with his backstory revealed, everybody wants him. He is also a very good-looking fellow, cream with apricot splashes. I've noticed that a lot of Americans prefer their tragic survivors when they're not *physically disfigured* by the tragedy.

Perry comes home with me. It's clear from the moment he walks in the door that he's not my pet, nor I exactly his, but that we are each other's soul sibling. That night he sits on the lid of the toilet and watches intently as I take a bath. I keep trying to detect a note of lasciviousness or judgment in his gaze. That's what I'm used to. But there is none.

Every 9/11 we stay in New York after that, Perry always loses his bearings. Going round and round the apartment in mad circles, as if chasing dust. Howling at the moon, whether it's visible or not. I've heard similar stories from people who took in 9/11 animals and, later, dogs and cats from Hurricane Katrina. Companion animals have scratches in their grooves too.

After ten months of successfully caring for Perry, I'm allowed to get Junior. Junior is a short-haired ginger and not nearly so good-looking as Perry, but infinitely softer (his fur, head, and heart).

The adoption group has outlined in detail how to introduce the cats to each other:

"You carry Junior home in the crate. You leave the crate in the middle of the room and keep him in there for a few hours and just let Perry sniff him."

The problem is, it snows on us whilst I'm carrying him home and Junior arrives in the apartment a sad, wet thing, and I'm not allowed to let him out. I cave and pull him out to dry him with a towel. Perry looks at me with a combination of shock and hatred.

Then I have to shut Junior in the bathroom for twenty-four hours so they can paw at each other under the door. This means I can't get in there to cut, and the bathroom is where I do my cutting. I have a day off and that breaks the spell, like going on a cleanse. Plus, Junior has a social-licking problem. He licks me. All the time. His tongue hurts quite a bit, but not as much as the razor. It's like being transferred to a halfway house.

Eventually, Perry and Junior sit at other ends of the sofa,

looking straight ahead, like guests at a dinner party who've run out of small talk. That's how they remain to this day.

The pet store told me a brick fell on Junior's mum and maybe a little shard landed on him because he's not all there. It's interesting because it makes him so loving. Not long after I get him, he vanishes and is brought back by another cat, who lives on the basement floor. That cat's owner said it couldn't stop batting at the storage closet, and that's where Junior was living, for several days. This is around the time of the Elizabeth Smart kidnapping. When Junior comes home, Dad sends me a reworked version of a *Time* cover of the miraculously returned teenager, in the veil she'd been made to wear. It's a pop-up cover Dad has constructed. When you lift the veil, instead of Elizabeth Smart's face beneath the veil, it is Junior.

"I am so happy to have him back," I tell Dr. R. "I wish I didn't have to have a boyfriend ever, ever again."

Famous last words.

CHAPTER 14

I MEET SIMON at a rooftop barbecue on the island of Manhattan. Everyone around us is wasted. I walk across the roof watching the sunset, knowing he is watching me. He spills a dot of guacamole on my white jeans. To show him I don't care, I take a palmful of guacamole and wipe it over the entire length of my leg. Mum will say I was an asshole whilst I was with Simon, but it's only events like this that corroborate her theory in my mind.

"Your husband is so wonderful with children," a partygoer tells me as Simon, whom I met an hour earlier, carries someone's baby stroller down the stairs. I look at her and say the only thing that seems right: "Thank you."

After that, though we are frequently separated by work, we never leave each other. Whilst I am working on my issues, he has buried his past, but he has buried it alive. Simon isn't white, and he doesn't want me to be either. It's summer, I'm tan, and when we meet he thinks I am Latina. I don't correct him.

"Fine," I say to Dr. R, "I'll go with that. So what?"

But when he realizes I'm not, this is a problem. I have to stay tan or he thinks his friends might judge him. After we break up I go bloodlessly pale. But first we have a one-year long-distance relationship. We meet every month in L.A., usually at the Chateau Marmont. We wanted each other like drugs. He'd tear and scratch at himself, thump his chest, on the phone. There was always a crisis, always a drama, hysteria.

We just wanted to consume and to subsume, have it all, to make it all go away. It was terrible. He'd talk about the common well of pain he felt we shared and how much he admires the Jews for the pain they've suffered.

We cut together, several times. Sometimes he goes too far, sometimes I do. I remember he calls Dr. R from the other side of the world. I am in the back of a car and Dr. R is on the phone, I don't quite understand how. It is the next day there. Or the day before. "Help me?" I ask, pathetic. Suck me down the phone and spit me out on East 94th Street.

"You're OK," he says. It sounds like he is convincing himself.

Back in New York, we have a disastrous session where I introduce them to each other.

I explain that Simon has yesterday refused to leave for a meeting unless I promised not to swim whilst he was gone. He didn't want other men to see my "perfect" body. It made me nervous, I tell him, because I would not always have this body, so it was wrong for him to focus his obsession on it.

Simon looks at the ceiling, sniffs, and cracks his knuckles. "I think you've misunderstood me. You have stretch marks on your arse and your tits sag. What I meant was that your body is perfect *to me*."

I look intently at the carpet.

Dr. R asks, "Are you OK?" But I can't answer.

I excuse myself to the bathroom. I lose it. I get it back together. I return to the office and knock. Dr. R peeps his head around the door. I can't look him in the eyes.

"Have Simon leave," I say.

Simon does. I can't look at his face as he passes me, but even his feet seem apologetic.

I sit back in the swivel chair. I can't look up.

"Emma?"

I am silent.

"Emma?"

If I look at the carpet, then I have not gotten myself into this situation with this man and I don't love him and I'm safe. I finally make eye contact. I can see he wishes he had not heard Simon's outburst. I've embarrassed him. Simon has broken some kind of fourth wall in this room. Dr. R takes a deep breath. Though it makes no sound, I hear his tic without seeing it. Finally, he speaks.

"This is not good."

He's never said that before. He looks at the door. I've asked him a million times if it's really soundproofed. But he's looking at it like Simon can hear. Simon can tell when I'm lying. "I know the rhythm of a lie," he says, and he does.

"This is a very angry man."

"Mmm."

Through sobs, I say the most redundant thing ever. "He really upsets me."

"That's why he said it. He felt cornered and he lashed out."

I listen to Dr. R. I don't just talk at him, because I can't talk, so I have to listen.

I leave East 94th Street. I go back to my apartment. I break up with Simon.

It's done. I'm free.

Ten days after we break up, I find out I am pregnant.

CHAPTER 15

——————————

I ALWAYS SEE MONICA LEWINSKY when I'm crying in West Village cafés, drinking ginger ale to tamp down my pregnancy nausea. She appears before me like a genie from a bottle. This is not hallucination. She never comforts me, but she does eventually ask for diet tips after we strike up a conversation. She pains me greatly. I would flash my thong at the president. Obviously I would. What she is, what she represents, young female sexuality, the fear of it, and then it genuinely does cause the downfall of the Western world. I feel a note of anti-Semitism to the "Ick, why her?" editorials. She is like Glinda, the Sad Witch.

There are victims, not just of murderers, like Chandra Levy, but of fucking and lust, of love. Poor Monica.

I remember what I was wearing when I met Simon and I remember what I was wearing when I aborted what could have become our child. The former was white jeans and a cropped floaty top with gold necklaces, rings, bracelets, and hoops. I was thinking I was a gypsy and could tell my own fortune, or a J. Lo, just Emma from the block. I rattled as I walked, but not so loud that I couldn't feel his eyes on me.

The latter I put a lot of thought into, laying it out the night before as if for school. As if I were my own mother. Or an echo back from a parallel universe where I was someone else's mother, protector of this thing that was making my stomach roil every morning from eight to ten and making my breasts ache every afternoon from three to five. That autumn morning at 9 a.m. I slipped on battered Converse sneakers, a thin orange T-shirt, jeans, a Marc Jacobs sweater with hearts on it—love, love, childish love that, for us, had not been contained in a perfect heart shape but had spilled, instead, into disappointment, rage, and jealousy and was now irrevocably broken just as the fetus materialized.

I was showing very early. Six weeks and you could tell. I wanted him to see it before it was stopped (the date was set in stone, my body shifting). "I bet you look beautiful," he said from the other side of the world. He was always on the other side of the world. "I do." So what? I knew from the start he was the first man I had let inside me because I loved him—however inexplicable it seemed to my friends and family, who only ever saw us fight—and not because I wanted to be told I was beautiful.

We didn't speak after that. I cried on the day, in the changing room, when I tied my surgical gown in the mirror. (Why a looking glass, why there?) "You look . . . young," said Margaret, my gynecologist, pulling tenderly at my ponytail. She was a deeply glamorous woman in her mid-fifties, perpetually in a tight skirt and high heels, amazing cleavage, blown-out red hair. That she asks her patients to call her by her first name gives her the air of every bad kid's one cool teacher. I always felt like a most unwomanly, unsexy waif in her presence, and now that suited me just fine because sex had gotten me into this mess. A holiday with a twenty-one-hour time difference had confused me and I'd screwed up my pill. When I first went to Margaret she examined my test and declared, "You are faintly pregnant."

"Faintly pregnant? Isn't that like being sort of a Nazi?"

"You are pregnant. And, since you don't wish to continue with the pregnancy, we have to wait a few weeks to operate."

And so I marked Bush's second inauguration by awaiting my first abortion. Truly, for me, it was no big deal physically. No, I am not sorry I did it. Simon suffered worse, I think, especially as he couldn't be there. Just as pornography makes women hate men every bit as much as it makes men hate women, abortion raises dreadful antiwomen feelings in men. Perhaps it is as simple as their lack of control over something they have helped create. But, by his own admission, Simon went absolutely crazy when I had the termination, even though he didn't want the child. "Hey," said Margaret. "I see it all the time."

My friend came out to stay with me, a woman the same age as me, going through a divorce. We lay in the curious post-summer sun and prayed for the rays to bleach away our sadness, our failure. I slept each night with my hands on my stomach. My cats, smelling not a baby but hormonal flux and drama, fought to sleep on my tummy. I talked and talked to the clump of cells. And they never once talked back.

I run into a skate-kid I knew vaguely around the time of my suicide attempt. He looks at me wide-eyed and I know what he's not saying is, "Oh, I couldn't remember whether or not she survived."

"No. Just pregnant."

If ever there were proof that our lives have alternative narratives, this is it. I would have a five-year-old child? Be in this same terrible relationship, stretched like taffy?

I know I will write about the abortion, and I do. While it's in me, when it's gone, the writing breaks my fall. I give a short script to the photographer Nick Knight and he gives it to the Italian actress Asia Argento and they make a demented short film. She leaves me messages like a sexy Italian version of Selma and Patty from *The Simpsons*: "Hi, this is Ah-see-ah." When I see the finished product, she has chosen to talk direct to camera.

She likes my writing because I seem unhappy. But there's a disconnect somewhere now. I am happier than my writing will let on, especially once the surgery has been scheduled. After all this abstract, pulpy love pain, here is something real. A list of postsurgical procedures to follow from the doctor. Friends who are required to be there to check you're still breathing.

"Your mom's coming over?" asks Dr. R, before I go in for the procedure.

"Yes."

He seems terribly sad. It's the first time I've sensed a paternal feeling from him. I am sad I've made him sad. I determine not to do that again.

I knew that having weeks to wait would give me time to fantasize about keeping it, letting it develop into a baby. And I did succumb to that fantasy. Where I was financially stable. Where I had a partner. Where the father didn't live on the other side of the world.

Shannon and Bianca were there for me. It was, in that it brought everyone who loved me together, from my friends to my parents, one of the most touching experiences of my life. But then I have the luxury to find inspiration in the pain because I am a middle-class girl with a tight-knit family.

I recovered fast, instantly. I woke up, had five minutes of slight cramping. I didn't throw up. Went home, got into bed, slept for twenty minutes. When my mum arrived from England an hour later, I was making Bianca toast.

For me, my abortion was an ending in that my relationship with the father could not survive it. He didn't want a child but he wanted me to want his child. I understand this: I didn't want a child but I wanted him to want my child. And we did. In a parallel universe. Which is not *Daily Mail* pictures of "This could have been a human being!" but something more abstract in its sadness. Our romantic tumult was a conversation between two adults. Declining to involve a child was my first act of protectiveness. It was sad. It was right. Our first, and only, act of being loving parents was not to have it. It was the only kind thing we had ever done for each other.

CHAPTER 16

———————

A MAN SITS DOWN next to me on an airplane to the Sundance Film Festival. It is 10 a.m., and he's been killing time at the bar whilst our plane was being cleaned. I might mind the smell of alcohol he carries to the center seat if he weren't my favorite playwright. His talent looms over anyone our age who wants to be a writer. It seems fitting that he is so immensely tall. After the plane ride, Loom sends me a copy of his new play and signs it: "If you don't think this play is brilliant, you must be mental."

We layover in Chicago but don't lay together. This is mainly because I come downstairs to the hotel bar in footie pajamas to look for him and find the lobby transformed into a nightclub. "Miss," snaps a bouncer, "that is *not* appropriate wear." Women are literally in fur bikinis. When I reminisce about our near miss, Loom frowns: "I was never going to sleep with you that night."

"Oh," I say. "I was."

"Oh," he says. "Tramp."

On returning to New York, I find Simon is in town and following me, this being my month off following him. I ignore him.

Loom and I go to dinner. What I don't know is that whilst I was out, Simon broke into my computer and read my old e-mails. One, from Loom, says, "Do you suppose we'll ever sleep together?" I know him well now and can hear his intonation. The intonation is akin to "Do you suppose the new David Lynch film will be any good?"

Loom and I go to see *Spamalot*.

The lights dim. And as they do we see that—Simon is sitting in front of us.

I understand that, because of me, the greatest playwright of our generation may be about to get punched in the face. During the opening number of the Monty Python musical. This is an unusual situation to be in. And I understand it is my life. Loom pulls himself up to his full height. Simon realizes that he wouldn't win this fight. Cut to several hours later: Loom has smartly removed himself from the situation, and Simon and I are in my bathroom. He locks the door.

"Shall we do it?"

"What?"

"Kill ourselves?"

I look at Simon. For the first time I see how much taller he is than me. It's strange, as a self-harmer, to feel afraid of someone harming you. I don't know what to do, and I remember the dream about chewing off your own foot to stop the rat from chewing it. I take the nearest razor and cut my stomach, deeply. The blood surprises him. It surprises me. He unlocks the door. We lie on the bed. I hold him to me because I am afraid of him. How often do we keep people close so they can't get in striking distance? I do not want him anymore and I will hold him until I can get him out and then I never want to hold him again.

CHAPTER 17

————————

THE NEXT DAY, Dr. R observes my stomach cuts. Like an actual doctor, which of course he is, though it's funny to me.

"Have you cleaned it out properly?"

"Yeah."

"And used Neosporin?"

"Bacitracin. I really screwed up." I am surprising myself when I add, "I wish I hadn't done that."

"You had a reminder."

He will never say: "You fell off the wagon." He always calls it "Having a reminder."

He adds, "It's over for a reason. You're looking out for yourself."

"I am?"

"Sure. I think it would be a very good idea if you would attend an SLA meeting."

I stare at him.

"You want me to join the Symbionese Liberation Army?"

He snorts with laughter. "Sex and Love Addicts. Anonymous."

"What? I'm not a sex addict!"

"You have patterns of love addiction."

"Yeah, but nice patterns. Like Liberty prints or something."

"Be serious for a moment."

"Yes, I have patterns of love addiction. But I'm a woman. Of course I do."

He scribbles. I prod him.

"You do what you like. I'm just saying it would be worth checking out."

I take the phone number he hands me.

"Why couldn't I make it work with Simon?"

He shakes his head. "You can't give unconditional love to somebody who hates himself."

On the subway from Dr. R, I listen to "Helplessly Hoping" by Crosby, Stills and Nash. The carriage is empty and I sing a little—I do all the parts myself—it's really rubbish—until six or seven girls get on the 6 train. They wear the uniform of a girls' baseball team. They are Latina. They have no make-up on. Their bodies are strong. They talk for half an hour and never once mention boys. They yammer and yammer, marveling at one another's performances. One starts talking about having light eyes and what it might be like, and I excitedly take off my glasses.

"Mine are yellow. I'm not lying. But you have to see them in the sun." They crowd round to examine.

"*She isn't lying.*"

"What's it like?"

I look at her. I think about it and, looking down, see I'm very tan and the sun has caused the scars that run the length of my wrist to rise and whiten. My arm would make an excellent hopscotch board for a mouse. The girl is waiting for an answer. I turn my arm over.

"It's good."

There isn't an Ophelia in the bunch. This is maybe a huge advertisement for the importance of girls doing team sport. They stand up, and as they crowd off the carriage, the leader calls behind her, "Look after your pretty eyes."

I promise the girl I will—promises to strangers being easier to keep—and it's only halfway up the block to my house that it occurs to me: I mean it.

Once Simon is gone, I start to become whole. I am as well as I have ever been, better actually. My decision-making is rational. Not impulsive. My house is tidier. I walk all the time. I am working my ass off to eat right, and some of my ass comes off. I'm weight training with a batshit-crazy Russian girl, who not only keeps me fit but also means that, in context, every Tuesday and Thursday at 11 a.m. I am irrefutably the sane one. Sounds privileged, but you can do it for free too, running along the river, not buying the chocolate cake. It's not a weight diet, it's a mind diet. Fish. Gross. Eat it. Vegetables. Gross. Drink them. Friends and strangers are appalled by my green concoctions I slurp through paper straws. I go to the light. I literally go to the light, moving to an apartment where, for exactly the same price, the sun is streaming in.

Writing from Czechoslovakia, my parents seem to be in an equally happy headspace.

Subject: Prague Report
Date: Sun., Aug. 27, 2006 4:55 a.m.

It was such fun when the Golem chased us across the Charles Bridge by moonlight. Luckily we both metamorphosed into giant insects, which saved us.

Love from
The Unbearably Light Beings.

CHAPTER 18

FOR THE FIRST TIME EVER, Dr. R doesn't have his full atten-
tion on me. He keeps looking at the phone, as if it were
about to do something. He excuses himself to take a call in
another room.

"I'm sorry."

"What's going on? Is it because I'm getting well and now
you don't find me interesting?"

"I had a patient almost die of an overdose this weekend.
At the Chateau Marmont."

"Eep. Like John Belushi."

"Something like that."

"Were they famous?"

"Emma."

"They were famous. Do the papers know?"

"Not yet."

It seems I keep this patient in the back of my mind, although I don't remember filing him for future reference
until he is sitting next to me at dinner two years later.

Airports make me want to reach out to ex-boyfriends. I was at the airport in Atlanta, Georgia, and I wrote the famous writer who'd had me twisted for years an e-mail. Saying to myself, there's no harm in a friendly note. But here's what happens:

> Hey,
> I went into the interfaith chapel. I paced up and down the terminal, saying "I'm going in." And when I finally went into the interfaith chapel, guess what I found? Some Muslims, texting. Then in the Quiet Lounge that says "Quiet" a man was on the phone saying "I didn't get a chance to tell you ..." and his voice catches and I'm thinking "It's the fucking Quiet Area." And I said, "Excuse me, sir, it's the Quiet Area" and I made a little prayer motion with my hands, in the manner of Mahatma Gandhi ...

I'm looking at it thinking, Is that a friendly note to someone I want to feel at ease as my friend, or is that a love letter to a lover? Into the letters-waiting-to-be-sent file it goes. And that's huge. I don't usually stop to consider things before acting. And I look at it again and see what I also mean to say is, "This is the rational area, this is the area for behaving rationally."

"I think," I tell Dr. R, "I'm really, a lot better."

I show him some hate mail I've received about one of my books.

"You know what's funny with hate mail? It always says 'Emma Forrest, I have read every single thing you have ever written and not once have I found any redeeming qualities.'

Wait, look at this: 'I have read *Thin Skin* three times now, and it is a piece of shit.'"

"Should have read it the fourth time," laughs Dr. R, "that's when it got good."

"So does that mean my experiences are a piece of shit or my writing is a piece of shit or I'm a piece of shit?"

"Emma, that's a lot of feces. *Thin Skin* is a tough one. It was a tough time."

"OK, but you know the J. G. Ballard quote? 'I want to rub the human face in its own vomit and then force it to look in the mirror'? I'm drawn to that because of my attraction to bulimia, right?"

"You're drawn to it because of your attraction to humanity."

"You think I'm really nice."

"You are."

"But I do these not-nice things."

"No, you do self-destructive things and sometimes forget the difference between things that are destructive to you and things that are destructive to other people. Just swear off the latter, which is against your nature anyway, and we'll deal with the self-destruction as and when it arises."

"OK."

"But it hasn't."

"Why hasn't it?"

"You got older."

"That's it?"

"The other part too."

"I got w—"

"You can say it."

"No, because then I have to take responsibility for it! Then I have to keep doing it, you know?"

He won't look away. "Say the word you were going to say."

"I got wiser?"

He blinks. "No question."

"Because I got older?"

"Because you did the work."

I frown. "It's really nice not being miserable."

"There are people who have no choice. You fell out of love with madness. That took self-awareness. And it took courage."

I smile at him. "If I'm Dorothy, are you the Wizard or the Scarecrow? Are you the horse of a different color?"

"I'm the Jew with a pad and pen. Don't worry about me. It's you. Time's . . ."

"Up."

CHAPTER 19

I SIGN AS A SCREENWRITER with William Morris and move to L.A. and have a "normal" boyfriend, Christopher, who is a schoolteacher and surfer. We homemake. It's really lovely. This was Heath Ledger's bungalow for a time before we took it. There is a love letter for Heath tucked into the wall when we move in. I don't know what to do with it. I hide it in a box of special things. One day Christopher, by happenstance, picks Heath up in the ocean and brings him home. I think about the letter and how I could possibly give it to him.

People are always asking, "What's it like being with Christopher, being with someone so good?"

It's just in his nature. Christopher, like most of the others I've been with, has recently given up alcohol. But under your sobriety is your nature, just as under your mental illness is your nature. Some people use twelve-step as a cover for their narcissism. Others really do want to change. I learn this from being with him.

His mom is the loveliest woman and helps make our home beautiful. It is a country cottage. There is no sadness here. Just hummingbirds. Perry is out of his mind with joy. He is a new cat. Junior is terrified of walking down stairs, and every time he needs to use his litter I have to carry him down.

One night I wake hearing rustling. Perry is next to me. I peer over the banister and see Junior in his box. From then on we never discuss anything, but he can do it. It's like getting well. He moves like a little old lady, but he can manage, and that's how I feel. You do it how you can do it; so long as it's getting done, you're OK. He comes downstairs backwards like how one might maneuver out of a tree. I did the same thing, myself.

Perry comes to me one day while I'm making tea. He has a lizard in his jaws.

"I've become incredibly interested in murder," he tells me.

"I thought you were all about killing mice."

"Yah, but that's so done. I only kill lizards now."

I do one terrible thing to Christopher whilst we are together. Christopher talks so glowingly of his ex-girlfriend that I start to obsess about her, until I track her down and message her on MySpace, but don't tell her of the link. We become friends and keep writing until I forget how I "knew" her.

I go back to New York to see Dr. R and I tell him what I've done.

"We're going to call Christopher right now and you'll admit it."

"Right now, right *now*?"

"Yes."

"No!"

"Yes. You tell him while you're here with me."

I hear Christopher take a breath from the other coast.

"Well . . . that's really weird." He pauses. Then he adds: "But I knew you were weird when I fell in love with you. The only part that matters is I want you to tell her the truth. It isn't fair to her." This is the kind of man Christopher is.

Dr. R is coughing a little and after we hang up with Christopher, he has a proper hacking fit. When he gathers himself I tell him a secret I've been keeping for some months now.

"Dr. R. I think I've transferred my childhood fear of my parents dying onto you. Lately, I've started worrying that one day, you will die. What does that mean?"

He stares at me, looks down at his pad.

"It doesn't mean anything." And then he tells me time's up.

CHAPTER 20

———————

IN CALIFORNIA, having composed the letter of explanation to Chistopher's ex, I hit Send.

I sit back that night and say to myself, "That was properly mental. That's borderline personality stuff and you don't want to be that."

Borderlines are what is commonly known as "evil." They enjoy causing trouble.

The ex says she is shocked and disturbed by my confession and that she needs to think. I never hear from her again. I am taken off her friends list. It makes me think, though: I don't lose friends as often as I used to.

Mum calls in the morning to tell me about the only cat she didn't like.

"It was at a house we'd rented in Edinburgh, and it was in the garden and it looked exactly like a snake."

"How can a cat look like a snake?"

"Well, it was long, and its body was the same width as its tail and it had no hair."

The next day a thought occurs to me and I call Mum.

"Is it possible that the cat you saw in Edinburgh was, in fact, a snake?"

She ponders this.

"Yes. I suppose it might have been."

There are still minor daily spazz-outs in my happy life with Christopher. For example, a regular trip down to the Laurel Canyon Country Store to drink Lilly and Spike's special coffee. When I get there, I see, tacked to the community noticeboard, an eight-year-old child's multi-pose audition card, where he's half-naked next to a lost-pet poster. The pet poster says: "Our beloved tortoise, Hokey Pokey, wandered off on Sunday. She has been with us for sixteen years. She is about a foot long." This is the worst moment of my life. The man at the deli in front of me has a terrible comb-over. This is the worst moment of my life. The sandwich I buy contains wilted lettuce. This is the worst moment of my life. When I get home, my cat refuses to sit on me. Of course the fucking cat refuses to fucking sit on me. He's a cat. And yet. This is the . . .

Still, Christopher and I keep homemaking and seeing movies and finding cheap eats in L.A. We go three times a week to Singapore's Banana Leaf inside the Farmers Market until they start giving us free mango juice and, in a coup, free rice crackers. We hike Fryman together. He runs back and forth without his shirt, all crazy and Catholic and self-flagellating.

When it unpicks, we calmly follow the cotton as it unwinds. He doesn't want to raise children in America and I do. I am second to the ocean, it is a religion I can't understand

and that I resent. It is the easiest, sweetest breakup. We go camping in the redwoods of northern California. We aren't going there to break up with each other, or maybe we are. We visit the Henry Miller Library. We eat incredible pancakes. We hold each other. Then he asks if I want to stay together and I say "no" and I ask him and he says he doesn't think we should stay together either. I cry my eyes out because he's so lovely and then we drive back down the coast holding hands and listening to Neil Young.

He waits until I'm not there to pack up his things from our home, leaving me a note like nothing I ever thought I'd deserve:

Emma, I will be forever grateful for your presence in my life. I am a much better human being because of you. The experience of loving you, living with you, was the greatest journey of my life thus far. You showed me an alternative to the man I was becoming. I know I still have much to learn, much to accomplish, and I know my future is bright.

I owe you the confidence I now have in myself. This is the confidence that could only come from the knowledge that a woman of your caliber loved me for who I am; for what you saw in me.

You are a great woman, and I mean that in the strongest sense of the phrase. You feel deeply, think deeply, and live deeply. I admire so much about you. Regardless of whether our paths cross again, know that I am actively wishing you success and happiness. I pray that you will once again be part of my life. But

if left with just the experience we've shared, I know
my life was better because of it.

That day, hiking Fryman Canyon, I come down the hill
and see a car with the license plate HEWZ VAN. It makes me
happy. It's cherry red. Maybe Hugh drives children and is
a FUN DAD. Or it's only him and he takes joy where he can,
this case being his car. I go home and do a phone session
with Dr. R. I try to tell him about HEWZ VAN and the joy it
brought me, but he keeps coughing.

"You're coughing. Do you have a cold?"

"I'm fine."

Then I take ten minutes telling him about Abba-Zabas.

"There's this candy called Abba-Zaba that I bought because I don't like it—it's chewy peanut-butter taffy—so I
figured I wouldn't eat it. Instead, I got completely addicted
to eating something I don't like."

I wonder if I knew this would be the last time we'd ever
speak, subconsciously, and that's why I filled the conversation with flighty inanities, so he'd know I was cheerful and
fine.

I don't have much to say. The breakup with Christopher
has been so dignified and respectful. I am ashamed to say I
wrap up my session with Dr. R before the fifty minutes are
up. I say he sounds sick. I say he sounds like he should go.
"I'll call you if I need you," I say, though I've a feeling it
won't be for a while. And then we hang up.

The next morning, I see Heath Ledger at the Laurel Canyon Country Store, with his little girl on his shoulders. His
skin is gray. He's buying Lilly's coffee from her cart. He

comes over and sits with me for a few minutes and I give him the half of the *New York Times* I'm done with and he says thanks and to tell Christopher he wants to surf this weekend. His daughter's wriggling to get going, and he heads off with his paper cup.

The crazy thing is: it turns out to be a magic coffee and it stays in his system so that, a week later in New York, he doesn't die and instead of taking an overdose at Mary-Kate Olsen's, he goes to Dr. R, who helps him get back on the wagon and somehow this means Dr. R doesn't die either, and everybody keeps making strangers happy, and all the children get to keep their dads.

CHAPTER 21

AT A DINNER, following a film screening, I am introduced to a man with long, flowing hair who is wearing a kaffiyeh. He looks like the world's campiest terrorist, but he's actually a movie star with a storied reputation, much of it here, at the Chateau Marmont hotel. In the candlelit garden we sit next to each other and talk and he admits later that every single thing he tells me is intended to translate as "I'm not like you've heard I am."

It works. Because it's true. This is GH.

GH is supposed to be really good-looking ("Of course," my father would say "he is *supposed* to be really good-looking"). But I don't see it. I see something . . . softly wounded, like distressed velvet. A touchable sadness he has.

Later I say: "You didn't try to shag me that night."

"I respected you too much."

"Oh my God," I answer, offended, "you only want me for my mind."

"Don't be daft!" he replies, "I only want to fuck ya!" He is the saddest man who's ever made me laugh uncontrollably.

He calls from a remote island where he's preparing for a role. Thus far it has been a barrage of texts, poems broken up into thirty little pieces. When he calls, it is because it is 5 a.m. and he has a yearning to hear "Skeletons" by Rickie Lee Jones. I cue it up and play it to him down the line. He takes a deep breath.

"I'm probably going to spoil it now. I'd probably better hang up now, Em, before you stop liking me."

I don't check in with Dr. R on this. I trust my gut, and tell GH, next time he texts: "I'm not going to get romantically involved with you. I think that you might hurt my feelings."

The reply is instant: "Ugh, just got a wave of nausea at the idea of ever hurting your lovely feelings."

Then he lands back in L.A. and is on the way over to my house.

It's raining very hard and he almost kills himself on the drive over texting his thoughts as he drives.

"Stop texting." I snap. "Just get here!"

"I just thought it would be safer if I remained your textual suitor."

He walks in the door, head bowed, paralytically shy. He is ashamed, because he comes bearing his own dinner, a Stouffer's low-fat lasagna frozen meal, trying to drop pounds for a role. He puts it in my freezer and forgets to ever eat it.

I make tea. We watch an old movie. Then we watch the rain for a long time. Then Junior creeps on the bed and GH introduces himself ("Hello, love"). Then I show him unseen pictures of James Cagney. Then there is nothing left to show him and it's well past midnight, so we decide to try to sleep. We lie in silence awhile. Even Junior holds his breath.

And then, with the feather-green darkness pressed against the windows, he puts his filthy fingers on my scrubbed hope face and says, in a tone that falls somewhere between optimism and regret: "If I kiss you, it's all over."

And then he does. And then it is.

CHAPTER 22

"I'VE BEEN SEEING SOMEONE you would probably consider inappropriate," I tell my sister.

"A neo-Nazi?"

"No."

"You didn't get back with Simon?!"

I'm getting impatient. "No."

Her voice becomes dark. "Not Russell Brand? Tell me it's not Russell Brand."

Since he is neither a neo-Nazi nor Russell Brand, the family is OK with GH, who is on a film set again.

Lonely in different time zones, we send the moon back and forth to each other. "Did you get it?" I ask.

"Yes, baby."

Whenever he comes home from making a movie, he brings me back strange things. My L.A. girlfriends, the ones who have been here too long, snipe, "No diamonds?" and I explain I wouldn't wear diamonds, never have. "Yes, but he doesn't need to know that." "He knows that," I say, and understand myself, whilst the gossips are asking, "Why is he *with* her?" Why he is with me.

He says I am Dorothy to his Cowardly Lion and that we must walk the red carpet together for his latest film, whilst imagining it's the yellow brick road. So flu-ridden that I am in bed reading *Eloise*, my favorite childhood book, I agree to go. He has successfully booked me for a gig, four months in advance. This pleases him so much, he spends the rest of the afternoon reading me *Eloise* in the voice of Daniel Day-Lewis's character from *There Will Be Blood*. He is absolutely brilliant. The Noël Cowardly Lion.

I try to think how Dr. R would feel about me walking the red carpet. Am I supporting my partner's work or am I permitting unwanted cameras into our relationship? What would he say? It's strange to try to speak for the dead. My scars have gone down, mostly. There's still a flesh flower on my upper right thigh, and I can tell from the nonchalant reaction of bikini waxers that they've become used to this sort of thing: girls who want to prettify and uglify, and cannot find a difference—like that hypothetical circle where communism meets fascism.

An hour into a phone call one night, GH, on the other side of the world, broaches a new topic.

"When I get back from this film, let's have a miniature human, that grows."

I freeze, look around my bedroom for witnesses.

"A baby?"

"Yeah, one of them."

After all this work with Dr. R, to get sane, to get whole, to be complete enough to support someone else. This is the conversation. I don't know what to say.

"If it's a girl, can we call her Pearl?"

"Pearl! My ego wants to fight it"—I can tell he's smiling—"since I didn't think of it. But that's perfect for her. Pearl it is. When I get home."

I summon again my invisible witnesses, Dr. R, my mum. And once they're both there, I ask them to give us a moment alone. I can do this myself.

"Do you just want me to give you Pearl? Or do you want me to stay too?"

He tries to answer. I hear his breath catch in his throat. The wait is interminable.

"I want you to stay. Em: I never want there to be a time when we don't share space."

He gets home late at night. It's unbearably hot and I'm sleeping downstairs on the daybed. I've passed out with the iPod shuffle on. He creeps in. I don't know how long he was in the daybed with me. When I wake up he says, "Guess what was playing when I got here?"

"Can't."

"'Darkness on the Edge of Town.'"

"Portent?"

"Yeh. Yeah."

He kisses me. As his tongue searches the back of my throat, there is a note I've never picked up before either because it wasn't there or because he hid it, or maybe he'd just never kissed me this deep. Fear. Of me, of himself. Of paying the cost for wanting things that can be found only in the darkness on the edge of town. He wants to tell me something. I can only feel him, in the dark. With his hand over my mouth so I can't answer back, he says: "I would rather die than not knock you up."

With his hand over my mouth, I answer him back, anyway.

INVENTORY: *Gifts*

3 × Pop rocks

1 × Kenyan Barbie doll

2 × Pig salt and pepper shakers

1 × Snow globe

8 × Goody hairbands

2 × PEZ dispensers

1 × Moose antler catapult

1 × Paddleball game

And that's all I need.

CHAPTER 23

———————————

A T-SHIRT ARRIVES BY FEDEX from a faraway film set. It stinks of GH but, even more important, is covered in a ballpoint love letter, his scratchy handwriting creeping across every inch of the cotton. It is an invitation, in verse, to meet him in Manhattan. He is as gifted a natural poet as anyone I can think of. He writes four, five, six a day, sometimes barely tasting them, like a compulsive eater.

So I meet him in New York. No one knows we're there, no one sees us. We never leave the room. I think about the secret voice you use when you make love, like the secret voice you use in a room with a psychiatrist. No one but that person will ever hear it. And here, we listen to each other, but we lock it in with touch, and the room vacuum seals it to stay fresh until we can breathe together again.

When he breaks the silence it is to say, "I want you to know that, when you get pregnant, nothing is going to change except your dress size."

And then we go our separate ways.

He doesn't like that my front gate doesn't close properly so, though he is on a film set thousands of miles away, he sends builders to fix it and make me a bolt lock for my front door. He doesn't like the way I can't open my windows at night because I don't have screens to stop the cats getting out. He sends the builders to make screens. He buys me an enormous Flann O'Brien book that I mean to read but end up using to kill a brown recluse spider.

I am always in the bath (in the womb) when his texts whir to life, long distance, late night. I bathe, I towel off, I go downstairs to the daybed by the French glass windows. We never stop texting. "Wait," I say one night, "a raccoon is staring at me."

"Don't be scared, baby! It's just me in my raccoon suit. I'll waggle my tail so you'll know it's me." It's been in the back of my brain all this time: GH reminds me of my father.

He decides that, for my birthday in December, we will go to Istanbul together (we pluck it from our gypsy fantasies), and when we've done that, we'll come back and make Pearl. When he's not talking about making love to me, he's talking about Pearl, and when he's not talking about Pearl, he's talking about our trip to Istanbul.

One night, for no good reason, I have the panics and fear it is over. I hold my tongue and put my phone under the pillow to hide it from myself. I settle down to write, and as I do, a parade of baby raccoons waddles past my window. I am soothed. "Thank you, GH!" I don't tell him about it but I thank him anyway. The raccoons come by every night at 8:20, until he comes home.

The TV, faded to blue, is on when I get there. He is on the sofa, naked and quite asleep. I watch him and stop myself from bothering him. I entertain myself as much as I can. It is a big house. I wander from room to room. I open drawers. I pick up a postcard with Venice on it. From the curlicue writing on the back I know it is a girl and feel instinctively he has caused her sorrow. I pace around the postcard. I do not look. I go to the bathroom and use one of her tampons. It has been left for me by "the first Mrs. de Winter." Finally, after letting him sleep another twenty minutes, I climb on top of him. He opens his eyes, smiles, and, looking straight into mine, says: "I missed you!"

When I get home the next morning, I open the e-mail about Dr. R. It has been sent to an account I rarely check, and has been there some time.

CHAPTER 24

———————

GH SAYS EVERYTHING he possibly can to help. He writes me poems. We talk for hours. And then there is nothing else he can say. So he sends me something instead.

He FedExes me one Werther's toffee.

When he comes home, he reads every single obituary of Dr. R. He lets me talk about him for days. He lets me cry. Though he tries to persuade me that Dr. R's keeping his sickness a secret was not a betrayal, it's a feeling I cannot shake, apart from when GH is physically shaking it out of me. Outside the bedroom, we bake a lot of cakes. We collaborate on rhubarb crumbles. We do most of it on his time clock, which means we're cooking around 5 a.m. and closing our eyes around 7:30 or 8 in the morning.

Around the time I find out about Dr. R, the newspapers find out about me.

We read obsessively the nasty comments. When you live with voices in your head, you are drawn inextricably to voices *outside* your head. Very often the voices work to confirm your worst suspicions. Or think of things you could never have imagined! There are only so many hours of the day to hate yourself. The outside voices are pitching in, volunteer shifts.

I am fat and ugly. GH is an unwashed manslut. We are pregnant. (They always say you're pregnant before you actually get pregnant, that you're living together before you've moved in, and that you're soulmates before you've said it out loud. It does take some of the joy out of it.)

I tell him my sister, having surveyed the Internet, has collated the comments into one conclusion: "You are having a fat ugly baby that's using GH to sell books."

GH grins. "That's only if it's a girl, love. If it's a boy, it's an unwashed anorexic who's using you to boost its intellectual credibility."

GH goes back to set. Mum, Dad, and Lisa come to visit me.

The kids' film *Kung Fu Panda* is being advertised on billboards everywhere, and one of the first things Mum says when she walks in the door is "I *do not* want to see the word 'Pandamonium.'" She shakes her head. "That is not what I've come here for."

Other things she does not want to see in L.A., and which provoke a vocal and vigorous reaction:

Pictures of Seth Rogen.

Nectarines from Whole Foods.

And the whole family gets cranky at the incessant beep of GH's texts.

—————————

CHAPTER 25

ONE OF DR. R'S PATIENTS finds out about his death from my blog. A middle-aged drug addict who went back and forth for treatment, he had been trying to get an appointment only to hear the message saying the office was closed.

His name is Mike and he writes on his own blog:

Depression sucks. Depression, accompanied by the death of the wizard who could work some magic and help make it go away, is even more awful. But shit happens and there is usually a reason for it.

The Great Wizard Dumbledore died before he could defeat evil.

But through his death Harry was able to marshal the wisdom and power to do it himself. Maybe there is a lesson there for Mike. Maybe its not the magic but the knowledge. My Dumbledore is dead and I'm sure his Phoenix has risen. Now its my turn to search for the knowledge to defeat evil. It's a great battle and maybe I'm truly the evil

*one who needs to be defeated, maybe not. But those lessons
are still ahead.*

*Today when I ran past 94th St., my metaphor of Hog-
warts, there is even a castle on the corner, I saw a ray of
light—Fawkes, the Phoenix rising.*

GH comes home and starts shouting, "Gypsy Wife?" and I
hide from him behind the sofa, just because. I'm planning to
burst out. "Gypsy Wife?" he bellows. And then I get scared.
Why have I hidden behind the sofa in the nude? It's a mad
thing to do. I'm mad. This isn't good. I should just stroll
out. Or I could stay behind this sofa forever and he'd eventually move on and I'd have to hear him make love to other
women on the sofa and that would be rubbish so I should
probably just stroll out now. He goes out into the end of
the garden calling for me. I come out, put on my clothes,
and arrange myself on the sofa. When he comes back I tell
him I was there the whole time and he just didn't see me.
Then we talk about shape-shifting, then we make love, then
we swim, then we do some reading, then we do some writing, then we bake a cake, then we watch a movie, then we
make love, then we go to sleep. Somewhere along the way
he says, "It's good we're not mad anymore," and I concur.

CHAPTER 26

KNOWING THE DEPTHS OF MY FEELING for the great man, GH arranges for us to fly out and see Leonard Cohen play in Lisbon, Portugal. At seventy-four, Cohen's on a comeback tour, after years of living up a mountain as a Buddhist monk, after years, before that, of alcohol and pain. The venue he's playing is basically a parking lot. Listening, eyes closed, GH wrapped around me, I carry R with me. I carry the wisdom of all Jews, of everything worth knowing. I listen to Cohen turning ugly things in on themselves, making them beautiful. I am, to a large extent, here because of Dr. R. I think back to that session when I told him about what happened in San Francisco. And I realize that this is the happiest night of my life.

I am turning this over and over like a pebble. I am so happy and I've been this way with GH for six months now and it's the longest I can remember. It's not mania. Is this mania? It's not. Is it needy? It's not. We don't need each other. We just really, really enjoy each other. And we're good together. We're good people together. And I have the funniest feeling. I can really, truly touch this all, this happiness, and the sadness too, I can trace all of it with my fingers. It isn't theoretical or distant. It isn't a facsimile. This feels like me. This is me. I love him, and, for the first time in a relationship, I also like me. Every time he says "I love you," I answer, "I believe you."

When we get back to the house we've rented in a little fishing village, GH arranges for my parents to come stay with us. Before they arrive, he spends a tormented half hour wondering whether or not to hide the Chekhov short stories he's been reading.

"I don't want them to think I've left it there on the table to try and get them to like me."

"Well. Are you reading the stories?"

"Yes."

"So leave them where you left them."

The very first thing Mum does when she walks in is look at the coffee table and beam: "Oh! People don't read the short stories of Chekhov nearly enough!"

As he helps her with her things, GH lifts my mum's sweater to his nose and turns to her. "I wanted to smell your sweater. I stopped myself."

"You can," she offers sweetly.

He takes me aside and whispers, "She's like amber, there's so much reflected inside. I just want to keep looking at her." He's right. That he understands, straightaway, how amazing she is makes me trust him more.

GH butters a digestive biscuit and Dad's ears prick up. "Are you putting butter on a digestive biscuit?"

GH looks guilty. "Yes. I say you should spread butter on everything until you find something butter doesn't taste good on."

Dad is delighted. His whole face contorted with joy—he has a triangle mouth like Eric Cartman from *South Park*.

They go off together into the night, ostensibly to fetch us dinner. After what feels like several hours, Mum and I start to worry. Eventually they return with a lovely Indian platter, which we devour. We package away leftovers, though we ate it all so fast we can't remember what anything was. Taking a Sharpie, Dad labels one carton "Mystery." GH scrawls beneath, ". . . wrapped in a riddle." Dad grabs the pen back. ". . . cloaked in an enigma." They smile at each other.

Washing-up done, Mum looks at GH: "You guys should go to bed before Dad says something terrible."

Dad's mind visibly whirs—there is so much tabloid fodder to pick from that he simply cannot choose. Dad leaps to his feet and, pointing at GH, bellows: "GH is made of cheese and jelly!"

From then on, when my dad talks about GH he says, "My boyfriend says . . ." but then one day I mention "Your boyfriend sends his love" and Dad snaps, "He is *not* my boyfriend, I am *his* boyfriend."

At the Spar supermarket, two nine-year-olds in Ronaldhino tracksuits follow us up the aisle. We catch them staring. "Don't mind him, GH, he's just a fat-head!" says one boy of the other. This, despite having, himself, the fattest head either of us has ever seen. The lack of self-awareness fills us with delight and we skip arm in arm into the night.

At a petrol station a mother pushes her little boy towards GH for a photo. The boy is twisting to get away. Why wouldn't he? GH is in a sartorial phase I can only describe as Bobby Sands does Dexys Midnight Runners. This child will always remember him as a terrifying vision from his nightmares.

"Love, he doesn't want to," pleads GH.

"You do!" the mother says to the boy.

"Love, he doesn't."

"Now you don't get any sweets!" we hear her yell at her kid.

GH puts his head in his hands.

To cheer him up, we go for his favorite thing—an aimless nighttime drive—and listen to "Postcards from Italy" by Beirut and "One More Cup of Coffee" by Bob Dylan over and over again. We have to hit replay before the song ends. "You do that? I do that," says GH, as he holds one hand on my heart whilst he drives.

GH wants us to road trip across America when he gets back. He asks me to book out Christmas and my birthday for the dream trip to Istanbul. He's decided that we should definitely start trying for Pearl in January. I want everything he wants.

"The only thing I know for certain," he writes me, "is that I want us to be family."

We're born alone and we die alone, but we get to travel with people along the way, and if, like Dr. R, you get lucky, you have a worthy consort. I feel as if I have that. I cannot express how much I admire GH, his intellect, his kindness, his sensitivity. Dr. R doesn't get to see it, but all our work has come to this.

CHAPTER 27

WE'RE AT A BUDDHIST RETREAT near the fishing village, lying on our backs in the clifftop grass. We have no shoes; our hair is splayed as if for a body search. The ocean is behind us. The view is spectacular. Luke Kelly singing "Raglan Road" is the voice in my head: "We tripped lightly along the ledge / of the deep ravine where can be seen / the worth of passion's pledge."

We lie beside each other, our fingertips touching, but don't talk. I think about Dr. R. How he left me, without telling me he was going anywhere. But how, before he left, he planted the seed in my mind of this patient who overdosed at the Chateau Marmont. After a while, I say as breezily as I can: "I thought it was you."

"What, baby?"

"Who overdosed at the Chateau? I thought you were Dr. R's patient too and that we were just leaving it unsaid."

He smiles. "No, love."

We are silent again. He is in his own world. My tears fall

very gently into the grass. I would like to go back, one day, to the retreat and see if anything is there, where I cried. I have never before, nor since, experienced such peace nor such love. Those twin hippie passwords of idealism. So shocking, the moments when they're actually tangible.

As we walk back through the retreat towards the exit, GH touches each colored Buddhist flag and, as he does, asks me: "Are you mine?"

"Yes."

"Are you mine?"

"Yes."

"Are you mine?"

"Yes."

"Are you mine?"

"Yes."

He has to stay in the fishing village, shooting for a few weeks. I am going back to America the next morning. Leaving our hotel for dinner, we happen upon a local arts and crafts store. Amongst the Aran sweaters and knit handbags is a fluffy pink coat for a baby girl, with attached rabbit's ears at the hood, and a soft flannel carrot sewn into one pocket. It's the cutest thing we've ever seen. GH gasps. "It's Pearl's rabbit coat."

"She would look sweet in it," I agree.

But there is a mist in front of his eyes. "I want to buy it for her now."

"Come back and buy it for her when she's actually been born," I reason.

He touches the coat. He strokes it. He feels it against his cheek. He paces back and forth, in and out of the store. We head back towards the hotel. He turns on his heels and goes back into the shop. He comes out with Pearl's coat in a plastic bag. I look at him. He looks at me and shrugs: "I was worried it might be gone."

At our hotel, a red-faced yelling man wakes us at 6 a.m. with his red face and yelling. The tray of breakfast we'd ordered is not nearly as sodden as his demands that GH cast his kids in the movie. I link any problem I have had since then directly to the foul yelling man, as if he were the sorceress entering the ball on my wedding night.

CHAPTER 28

———————

"YOU KNOW THE THOUGHT of coming home to you and starting our life and making our family is what's getting me through this shoot?"

I have been in Los Angeles, waiting so long for GH to come home. I count it off in the Sunday *New York Times*, which we read together in bed at my house (for some reason we always get up and go to my house to read it) after buying coffee from Spike and Lilly's Laurel Canyon stand.

He knows my mum has mailed me a copy of my suicide letter because I'm writing about Dr. R, and wants to be with me when I read it. I ask what he wants for his homecoming dinner and make him the agreed ceviche and a passion-fruit cheesecake.

He texts me from the plane to say he'll be in my arms in a few hours and our life together will begin in earnest. Then he turns off his phone and the plane takes off.

I have a ridiculous red tasseled burlesque costume, and I decide to sit on the wall outside my house and wait, like

Penelope looking out to sea for Odysseus, only spanglier. At the last minute I am too cold and decide it would be better to wear something with easier access. I put on a T-shirt dress.

His plane lands.

When he arrives at my door, he is shaking like—they say "a leaf" but it's more like someone in need of an exorcist.

"Are you OK?"

"No. I'm not."

"Let's go upstairs."

We lie on the bed. He looks at me.

"I think I need space."

"OK."

"OK?" There are tears rolling down his face.

"It's OK."

I keep saying it over and over whilst I stroke his head— "It's OK, it's OK"—because I have no idea what is going on. He puts his head in my lap and his shoulders heave. "Thank you. Thank you."

He lies there a long time.

"Em, you're taking this so well."

He looks like hell, like something you'd find in the plughole after Meatloaf washed his hair in your sink.

"You need space," I say back at him, wondering where he's put Pearl's coat.

"I need all the space."

A thought occurs to me. "Did you want me to have Pearl because you thought if we had a baby, you wouldn't be able to leave? Is that why you wanted me to get pregnant?"

"Maybe. That might be true." He can't look at me because he is crying so hard.

"Eat the ceviche."

"What?"

"Eat the fucking ceviche you had me make."

I imagine, when he is an old man, looking back on his life, at the breakups that litter his library floor like books fallen from the shelf, "Eat the fucking ceviche" will be one he thinks he must have read wrong. But it is what I say.

He sniffs, wipes his face, smiles weakly. "OK. If you'll share it with me."

We eat from the bowl. "This is the healthiest thing I've had in months."

"This is what love should be like: what we have," he says, gobbling down the dinner I made. "This is the standard we'll both have to hold out for when we're next with someone."

And it's crazy because here we are, this is it, you don't leave the path to find the path. This is what he says we should look for. I don't understand any of it.

I lock myself in the bathroom. I call from under the door: "You can go now."

"Em. Please let me in! Em!"

"I'm fine. Please leave now."

"Have you cut yourself?"

"No."

"Are you going to?"

"I don't think so."

"Promise me!"

"I can't."

This is where my cat gets shut in when he's been naughty. I curl up on his mat. From my vantage on the naughty mat, I can see, through the bathroom window, GH leave through my door and then my gate. I hear him turn on the car (he sits there for some moments) and then I hear him drive away. Still, I wait on the mat like someone who's unsure whether or not their attacker has left.

As I'd heard his footsteps down my wooden steps, I'd cleared the phlegm from my throat and called out loud: "Take the cheesecake."

"OK."

"And take the suicide letter."

His voice falters here. "OK."

CHAPTER 29

4 March 2000

Mummy

Daddy

Lisa

Please forgive me
I have had such a happy life with you
Mud lies down and goes to sleep now.

I love you always.

I will protect you always.

CHAPTER 30

I NEED DR. R more than I ever have, but instead, I have to get through this breakup myself, like normal people do. Only I'm not normal, he's not normal, and this is not a normal situation. GH and I are in his house watching *Harold and Maude* and then *Moonstruck* and then *Cleopatra*. I look at Liz, look at Burton. Have you ever felt that you don't truly taste the chocolate you're eating until you get to the last square? That's what the weekend is like. He's watching *Cleopatra*, saying, "That setup took ages to do and it wasn't worth it. See that part with the birds? Three days that would have been!"

He does a week's work in Santa Fe, and I imagine he will come back with Native American jewelry and an apology. Instead: "I got you this."

INVENTORY: *Bag of gifts*

2 × *Vintage* I Dream of Jeannie *salt and pepper shakers*

1 × "Dads! Refusing to Ask for Directions Since 1932!" mug

1 × Comical George Bush fridge magnet

I look at it. The context is off. The love of my life brought me a bag of useless crap.

After that, I found a letter to my website that I'd ignored (which I don't often do) because it described a portrait the writer had painted of GH. I stop reading there. She resends it and I read it this time. GH looks very much like her little brother, she says. She hadn't much interest in GH until her brother died of a heroin overdose and then he spoke up about addiction. She misses her brother. She found his body. "I'm not crazy or dangerous, just a bit eccentric and lonely." It breaks my heart, her self-awareness. I know that feeling, inside sadness, seeing it, being able to articulate it calmly and clearly, and it doesn't make any difference. I know the woman's painting is just sitting there, and I think about picking it up. Not now. Not now.

GH leaves two more things on my doorstep late one night. Music he's made me. To draw me in. And sage, he says, to burn him away.

You can't do that, contribute to my exorcising you. It's like giving yourself a nickname.

Because they don't know that it's over, his online fan community continue to say that I'm fat and ugly. I have felt that I was fat and I have felt that I was ugly and there's something both horrifying and exhilarating about seeing it said by strangers. Seeking out the worst he can find, GH, himself, googles exotic permutations of his name:

GH + Talentless + Cunt

I look at the comments about us compulsively and though I understand that reading them is a version of self-mutilation, I can't figure out how to stop. Some veer into Jew territory and I find myself longing for the days of good old-fashioned handwritten anti-Semitism. The online fans begin to actively wish for my death. "Maybe we'll get lucky and she'll take an overdose of lithium," says one. The sentence ends with a smiley face icon. One hasn't lived until one has experienced death threat by emoticon.

Soon enough, they have done research that links me to Dr. R and are speculating that I am a cocaine addict. It kills me like nothing else that they should write his name. But . . . why am I here?

Why am I listening? Because some part of me, even after all his work, still doesn't know which voices are real or not?

If Dr. R were here. If Dr. R were still alive. My mum is beside herself, more than I've ever seen her. I don't know what to do, or whom to turn to, so I write to Mike, Dr. R's addict.

Emma,

Being an addict and not a recovering one at the moment, but having many times been in rehabs and recovery, one of the AA lessons drilled home is never to take another addict's inventory. In other words, I can't decide what someone else is doing right or wrong. I can only speak to my personal experience which may or may not be true of another's.

I never lie—I am a blatantly truthful person about almost everything. My addiction (or disease as some call it) always lies. The addict in me will say or do almost anything to use. It hates the person who always tells the truth so it lies for me. I can almost hear myself saying "the voices came."

I have had very good relationships with women, the addict always fucked them up. I fall in love quickly, its a high that rivals drugs for a while. I have never cheated, I am sexually monogamous, but I always cheated with drugs before the relationship fell apart. I was married to my enabler (someone who has never even had a drink), got divorced when my behavior became dysfunctional enough to overpower our codependence, had some decent recovery time, got into relationships with great women, the addict always fucked them up sooner or later and have been back with my original wife for quite some time, enabling and codependent as ever. I actually began seeking out Dr. R a few weeks back for a return engagement because I was becoming dysfunctional enough to overpower our codependence again. Things have calmed down but this is not a healthy process, for either one of us, but I need her as my best friend.

Addicts need best friends, healthy people need healthy relationships.

I hope my personal experiences provide some insight into my addictive behavior. I think Dr. R might sit back in his swivel chair, look up from the manila folder on his lap (I always wondered what those little tick marks he was

*making meant), and with a knowing but concerned look
on his face, suggest a visit to AL-ANON to hear some
experiences of people who have had relationships with
addicts.*

Mike

CHAPTER 31

_____

I'M SUDDENLY AND UNNERVINGLY PANICKED by me.

The smell of my armpits.

The scent of myself on my fingertips after I've masturbated.

The perfume of my hair on the pillow.

Your lover says, "This is what you're like and this is what you're like," and you giggle and say, "I don't know what you mean!" And after they've gone, then, then you know what they mean. And there's no one to share it with.

It's only a heartache. It isn't a tragedy. A tragedy would be losing the father of my children to cancer. This I wrestle with the hardest. There are thirty-one flavors of pain, like Baskin-Robbins in hell. Am I allowed to feel pain at a breakup? When Dr. R's wife and children are going through his loss?

Spotted weeping at Shabbat services, I am called to the office of my rabbi. I tell the story, my embarrassment at feeling this loss so hard when it follows on the heels of Dr. R's death.

Rabbi Wolpe shakes his head. "Love is extremely serious. I don't think this is trivial."

A freezing fall in Manhattan and I find it hard to go back to New York, and especially to meet people on the Upper East Side. Within a fifteen-block radius, there are two rooms where I took my skin off. No one ever knew. In one room I talked and talked to a wise man in high trousers. In the other, there were hardly any words, just a skeletal man covered in fresh bruises, kissing a woman with curves and fading scars.

I am in New York for the honor of lunch with Dr. R's widow, Barbara. We meet at Sarabeth's, around the corner from his office. She is blond, pretty, clever as hell. To match her sunshine hair, I eat yellow foods. First I eat an omelet and then the lemon ricotta pancakes from her plate. I figure, if I just keep eating, I won't cry in front of her. If I don't cry, I can also stop myself saying, "What happened? Why didn't he warn me?"

She smiles as I eat her food.

"We were together twenty-seven years. Carpe diem was our motto. He was someone who did believe, in his heart, in living, and we always did, and we kept doing it after the diagnosis."

She pushes her remnants around the plate as if, were it to fall in the right order, she could say the right thing to make me feel better. Even in her grief, she is thinking of his patients.

"He gave his patients a sense of confidence, no matter how messed up things were. He was that positive. When he got the diagnosis he said, 'Life is rough but we fight this, we get through the chemo and get on.' It never occurred to him and so it never occurred to us that he wouldn't win. The end was a big shock."

Getting out her handbag, she brings a pile of books to the table. "These have been coming for you." I look. They are addressed to me, Dr. R, and GH. There are sprinkled with photos clipped from magazines of me and GH together.

"Do you know what these are about?" she asks.

"It's just a crazy fan."

"I don't understand."

"I was dating this movie star . . ." I stop, because I feel like I'm explaining a fringe subculture. Transgender. Plushies. Actors.

We hug goodbye.

As I ride the 6 train home with my stalker books, I think how strange it is that Dr. R and GH have finally intersected, not at all in the way that I wanted. And I think of Barbara, her parting words before I head into the station.

"I always tell my kids and I am telling you: you can have this kind of love. It's like grabbing the brass ring at the carousel. You can have it. You just grab it. Of course the problem with having that love . . ." The train picks up speed, her voice in my head trails off: "is that you can lose it too."

CHAPTER 32

I GET AN E-MAIL NOTIFICATION of dispatch from Love Fifi underwear. "We are so excited you found us. We are going to take care of you, now and forever."

It is very nice of the underwear to assure me like that, but it is startling. I don't want promises. Not from anyone.

I notice the hand cream by my bed says "Apply generously" and I say out loud, "Fuck you, hand cream!"

I see *O, The Oprah Magazine* on stands and though she usually poses in different happy ways in happy colors, this month it seems like the "O" is for Ophelia, who is floating down the cover on her back. How to repair love *and* gowns stained by drowning!

A raccoon walks by my window. But there are no more portents, no coincidences, no signs. It is just an animal, rabid, fiercely clawed. It's just trying to survive.

I feel the waters rising up around my heart. They don't stop. This is my last breath, this is my last heart. I'm searching frantically for an air pocket.

I have sex with a guy who saves my cat from being stuck up a tree. A Rottweiler chases Perry almost to the top. It's a sweet Rottweiler, but Perry knows the harm of which it's capable. "Can I try to get him?" asks the man, a passing friend of my landlord. He shimmies up with ease and gently talks Perry down.

I go in the house to find a thank-you present. I can't find anything good so I give him my vagina. He is very, very tender to my cat. He is rough with me. Doesn't it *at least* go: he saves my cat from a tree . . . then we talk about Barack Obama . . . then we have sex? No, not so genteel a preamble as that. It means less than nothing and within twelve hours it means everything. It is reckless and this means my meds are off. That is where I am again. I was trying to break a spell. It did not work. I said it wrong. It took me back in time instead.

Perry comes down from the tree filled with ennui. He has four mouthfuls of food and gets bored. Doesn't want to play outside. He just wants to be next to me, warm flesh against warm flesh, and that breaks what's left of my heart.

The cat rescuer comes back for me, once, twice. We don't know each other's number, he just appears. Each time I am caught unawares and wearing something more schlumpy, bizarre, and unflattering than the last. Like I have on a poncho and worms coming out of my eyes and one of my arms is made out of Dudley Moore. One day, I swear to G-d, I have on underwear my sister made printed with Jon Stewart's face and also, unfortunately, period stains.

On Halloween a beautiful bisexual squeezes my breasts and a man asks me out and each time this happens I feel crushed because it's the wrong one. We are three minutes from GH's house and I am wearing a Snow White costume. And I cannot go to him.

I remember I am on his video card. It was real. I rent three videos and resolve to keep renting every week, just like Joe DiMaggio putting roses on Marilyn's grave each birthday. Only less beneficent and more self-serving.

When people say, "He *is* a really good actor," I feel strangely proud.

I ask my landlord, Scott, if I can paint the downstairs of the guest house. It's depressingly off-white and chipped. He walks by and I'm on a stepladder huffing and crying and spreading paint.

"What are you doing?"

"Painting. You said it was OK."

"You didn't ask if you could paint it pink. Emma! You painted the fucking house pink!"

I'm huffing and crying and the paint is on my hands and in my Jew-fro and the house is indeed an absurd Pepto-Bismal pink.

"EMMA!" He gathers himself. "You are so damn lucky you're depressed right now."

INVENTORY: *Songs that are not about love, lust, longing, or loss*

Neil Young—"Rockin in the Free World." That's it. That's the only one.

I have migraines constantly. The sheer amount of migraine medication I take knocks out the effect of the psychiatric medication. I'm using it to sleep at night. I see *Synecdoche, New York* and I don't understand why Charlie Kaufman has made a film about me and GH. So. I am disassociating. Conditions are perfect. It is almost the exact perfect storm as the first time.

I look at the blue sky and trees and see places to hang. I used to look out my apartment window in New York and see places to fall. Where would my body land? Which branch would I choose?

Around 1 a.m. there is a pop from the kitchen and raw sewage rises up from my sink, and does not stop. It's like the Amityville horror. I keep cleaning it and it keeps coming. The stench is unbearable. I have returned the house keys to GH. I look around my kitchen in wonder. Everything has turned to shit.

I text GH. I tell him what has happened. He does not offer me a space in his paradise. He wishes me luck with the plumbing.

Have you ever seen *Mulholland Drive*? Laura Harring and Naomi Watts meet and fall in love and then they go to Club Silencio and they cry at the incredible singer, and then they come home and Naomi walks out of the room to get something and when she comes back in the room her lover is gone. She's just walked out of the room. And Naomi's life becomes a totally different movie. That's what it feels like.

As I hike to my iPod, "Raglan Road" rolls down Laurel Canyon: "That I had loved not as I should / a creature made of clay."

I bump into the cat rescuer one day when I am hiking my local hillside. He kisses me. I start to cry. This deters him not a jot.

"Um, my mentor died and then the man who'd asked me to make a family with him woke up one day and left."

"Your energy is overwhelming. It overwhelmed him."

"That's very kind but I don't think so."

He traces his finger up my thigh, under my skirt, and into my underwear.

He looks at me and says, "What I'm doing is not about sex."

"But it kind of is because now your finger is inside me," I say, like I'm naming that tune on a game show.

"No. I'm just trying to change your flow of energy."

I pull away from him.

"I understand that by finger fucking me at the side of a major highway you're only trying to be kind. But . . . it just isn't all that helpful."

That fitful night, I dream that Bob Dylan does abortions as a sideline. I am pregnant with Pearl and GH does not want me to get rid of her, but I figure if Bob does it, GH will be distracted by asking him questions, like "Tell me about when you and Emmylou Harris sang 'One More Cup of Coffee.'" It works. Bob Dylan gets to perform the abortion.

CHAPTER 33

ELECTION NIGHT 2008.

On every TV, there is this beautiful man who worships his wife, who tells us again and again he would be nowhere without her. Everywhere I look during this breakup, it says "HOPE." The audacity of hope. The stupidity of hope. The self-delusion of hope. Here's the truth: hope is, generally, a very poor strategy. I start to think about the audacity of despair. Am I brave enough to say this: *this* is a thing worth killing yourself for. If it wasn't, why would it be a leitmotif of literature, cinema, and opera for all time? Aren't clichés clichés for a reason, because they're true?

GH always loved how knotted and messy I was, that my hair and heart could not be tamed. "It's like fucking Medusa," he marveled. Now I am a classic of Greek verse, with her esteem flatironed. Just another girl, just any girl. This breakup has rendered me a Medusa afraid of her own snakes.

Barreling towards rock bottom, I reach out to GH, tell him things are not good and I would like to speak face-to-face.

He does not reply. For two days I roil in shock, knowing that he will. But he doesn't. Finally, an e-mail, cool, saying he's "glad I'm doing well," no mention of what I've said. It's as if he can no longer acknowledge the love he felt or the pain I am in. I have been dismissed. I don't think I was smarter than or as beautiful as the other girls he did this to. It's just that I was me. It was all I had.

I repaint the pink of my guest house, do something called a stain. Now it's closer to, well, red. 3-D. A bad trip.

Accepting the presidency, Barack introduces "my best friend of sixteen years, the love of my life, Michelle Obama" and I think I will pass out. That, right there, is love in action. When I go home, I try to fix on the happy mental image of little black girls playing jump rope on the White House lawn. Instead I keep thinking of Jesse Jackson. He's in the audience, crying so hard, he has his finger on his lips like a woman. That is how I cried all day. I cut the picture out of the newspaper in the morning and really stare. We are making the same face but me because I am despairing and Jesse because he is rejoicing and each of us is trying not to crumble with the emotion. Later in the day I decide he is not crying about the historic nature of the presidency; he is crying in the same manner and for the same reason as I: because GH has wooed him only to let him down horrifically, and he feels like an asshole for being taken in. He is looking at Barack and Michelle and thinking this is the greatest day of his life and the worst and he doesn't know what to do. That's the real reason Jesse Jackson was crying at the inauguration.

GH was addicted to me and now he has gone cold turkey. He used to send me fifty texts a day. And now he is ignoring me. It's like I was once his Barack Obama. And now I am John McCain, conceding defeat like a sad-face sock puppet, knowing I have sold the best of myself. He, my electorate, not only does not want me, he actively feels pity.

Weirdly, the writer with the famous words and love life, the one who had me in knots through my sessions for years, he's the only one I confide in. We're having dinner at a fancy restaurant and I'm in a pretty dress and I'm having a good hair day and L.A. is twinkling in our view and we're guessing the special. I ask him about the year he was in the tabloids for taking crack and he says, "Emma, please, you don't take crack, you smoke crack. Have a little respect."

We laugh and then midway through telling a joke my tears plop into the salmon, which is quite moist enough as it is.

"I'm not crying."

"Emma." He puts his hand on mine.

"It's OK because I'm not crying."

"Emma. Talk to me."

We've gone years without talking.

I tell him about how I think I've lost my faith. And how I can't stop writing because I don't know how much longer I can hold on.

He clasps both my palms in his. There's salmon on his jacket sleeve.

"Emma. You're just *really sad*. And you're right to be."

Everything he could never be for me when we were "involved," he redeems a thousandfold that night.

I adore him and he adores me and I don't care who he dates, I want him to be at peace and he doesn't care who I date, he wants me to be at peace. Given time, love can take on the most surprising shapes. I tell him this.

"It would blow Dr. R's mind that you're an anchor. You were so dangerous! He was so nervous about the damage you could wreak. I said, 'But he's so hot.' Do you know what he said? 'Hot, like crack cocaine.'"

He laughs, puts his head in his hands. Pulls his head back up, still laughing.

And it's the proof I have in action that distance can change everything, turn something ornamental into something healing, like watching a snow globe become a hot-water bottle.

He drives me to my door and watches to make sure I'm safe, as I get out my key to open the security lock that GH installed.

I am greeted by a sight that is amusing to me now. I kept hiding the T-shirt on which GH had penned that love poem, and wherever I hid it, Junior kept finding it and dragging it out, and I keep finding him making feline love to it, as he is this evening. I take away the shirt, one last time, fold it inside two bin bags, and place it at the bottom of my laundry bin, which, for some reason, Junior is frightened of.

When GH asked if he was mine, tears in his eyes, I think he knew what he would do, what he would have to do, and he was mourning us. He was mourning us the whole time, as I mourn Dr. R now.

Understanding this does not help.

Late the next night, I say to the man who saved my cat, as he undoes my blouse, "I want to die." I look him in the eye as he unzips my jeans, and I say it again. "I only want to die." He thinks that I am role-playing. He puts his hands around my neck and squeezes. Hard.

I lock myself in the bathroom with my BlackBerry, as I did the night GH left, and wonder, if I called him, would he rescue me from this. I look at his number. Please come and get me. Please kick this man out. And I know that if I called . . . he would not answer.

So I go back to the bedroom and let the man squeeze his hands around my neck again. This is not who I am. But I am here. So this must be who I am. His thumbs press into my throat. I wonder if he will go all the way.

CHAPTER 34

NOW THAT GH IS GONE, I feel like I'm a senior citizen who gave away her life savings over the phone. And this is the crux: I never in my life believed in someone as much as I believed in him. The shame is overwhelming.

Brushing past my leg, a velvet shark, Junior goes into my clothes closet to take his thrice daily nap. I go to the bathroom, find my bottle of pills, and then follow him in, right into the back, so I won't be found. Junior snuggles down. I take three pills, and then two more.

I count out the rest of the pills. There are more than enough. I have that weird moment—I had it the last time—where I have a headache and worry about taking two from the bottle, will I then have enough left to kill myself?

I am nearly thirty-two now. If I do it this time, it has to work. If it doesn't work I will most likely have to leave this guest house. I have bad credit now, nothing will ever be as nice as this, my cats are happy here.

There is no note. I have nothing left to say.

Junior crawls onto my chest. I had hoped that one of them would. That I wouldn't go alone.

In the back of the closet in which I'm curled, I find a high-heeled shoe I've been missing for a year. Junior has put a toy rattle mouse in it. Pleased to see it, Junior wakes, grabs it in his little jaws, and goes into the bathroom. Uncurling myself, I follow him.

He settles down on the mat. I run a bath and put the remaining pills on the windowsill. I lie back in the water, my hair floating wet behind my broken mind. Through the slats of the blind, I can see the trees and beyond them, I can see that the moon is full, our moon, the one we'd send back and forth to each other. "Tonight is perfect."

Then I hear a voice.

"Just wait," says Dr. R in the form of Junior, his orange paws up on the side of the tub, pulling his head over the edge, peering at me like a meerkat. "Just wait."

I'm talking to the air. Seeking solace in a cat. Noting portent in the random.

If I do this then Dr. R's death will have been for nothing. I hate it when Beyoncé wins a Grammy and in her speech thanks G—d. He didn't have time to help out in Darfur but he made sure you won an MTV Moonman. I know Dr. R left behind much bigger things than me. I know it. I know that I was not his primary relationship. But I was one of them.

The gap he left in front of him was watching his children grow up, was growing old with his wife.

All the girls offering me their ear now are younger than me. Ali is twenty-seven, Elishia twenty-eight, Natalie twenty-seven. Danielle is twenty-five and going through the same thing. I do not have the heart to tell her that the best advice I can give is that she will survive it and go through it again. And that it will be infinitely harder three years later, and five years later, and eight years later it may feel insurmountable.

"Pearl, Pearl, a pearl of a girl." I sing-song it with each little white pill. It's like a madrigal: pill, pearl, tear, pill, pearl, tear.

"We'll call her Pearl," said GH, "because her loveliness is self-created through her own intense willpower."

Sifting through the wreckage of my future, I wish I could be more like my imaginary daughter.

Of course there are questions of addiction patterns, of course he freaked out. Of course it's nothing to do with me. But none of that matters. He loved me and now he doesn't. I was everything to him and now I am nothing. I am closing my clamshell around myself.

Irregular Pearl.

I make a necklace from the pills. Pop one in my mouth, then another, swallowing bathwater as I go.

Junior is purring, loud, a Tibetan chant of the dead. And then I hear Dr. R, and look down at Junior: "Emma Forrest . . ."

No. I didn't dream this life. These incredible highs. The terrible lows. I want to be a cheerleader in . . . in . . .

"Where?" says Dr. R, cat-faced, injecting logic.

"In Minnesota."

"It's cold there."

"Yeah."

"Better to be a cheerleader here. There's blue sky."

"There is blue sky."

I don't understand why GH stopped being my husband. "I didn't stop," he wrote, the week of the breakup, "I am your husband. Always." "But you're not here." I see the ghostly chorus of other lovers who came before me, the other women he walked away from overnight. I wasn't the first. I won't be the last. I am a pearl strung on a necklace.

Junior nudges me, bats at my toes in the water.

"No one ever loved you like GH. And no one ever took it away so completely. But it's here. Look around. The spider under the Flann O'Brien book. The gate that finally closes. The lock on your front door. In small but important ways, he made your house safer to live in."

"I love you so very dearly," said GH, again and again on the phone, and though it makes no sense, I answer "I know," because I do.

Junior smiles: "People can only do what they can do."

I brush the rest of the pills into my bath. I am surprised when they sink straight to the bottom. And then, I guess, the coating comes off because the water starts to turn red. To a bystander, it looks like I am bathing in what might have been. I look. And I look. This simply isn't me anymore.

I get out of the bath. I pull the plug. I scoop up the coat-less pills, stripped to their white undergarments, and put them back in the bottle.

Four hours later, my landlord comes by. Four hours: probably would have been saved. Might have died. Would have had liver damage. Would have been kicked out. I go to the door, my clothes covered in cat hair from lying in Junior's closet nest. But Scott doesn't notice.

"EMMA! You painted the house red!"

"Sorry!"

"It's like we're in a dissected human organ. Emma! You painted the house into your broken heart."

I go upstairs, close the closet door, and sit on the bed, in my battered Converse and shame.

"I miss you," I tell the air to tell Dr. R, "so much."

The air passes it back: "I know."

The bottle of pills goes back in the cupboard, for another time, another lover, another life. Or just, as needed, for headaches.

CHAPTER 35

————————

I CLEAR OUT EVERYTHING of his. Every book he sent, every love letter, every poem, every piece of jewelry, the framed Tiffany photo he gave me to keep him safe when he was away. At some point, I happen to open the freezer and find, in the back, the Stouffer's low-fat frozen lasagna he brought with him the first night he stayed. Something tells me not to throw it in the trash. A voice in my head says I must take it down to the garden where we had made love so many times, and bury it there. So I do.

My window of reason is swinging. Suicides are so tragic because nothing interrupted them. I recognize that I need to get my medicine levels checked. Barbara suggests Dr. K, the only problem being he is in San Francisco. Ever since "the incident," at sixteen, that town has been my "Don't drive through Texas."

SB and Teeter were with me ten years ago for the first suicide. It's like Vatican II, this new one. New resolutions. We forgive the Jews. Many regretti. My mother will fly in and meet us there. On the long drive north, SB wants to listen to drippy American music and I want to listen to British melancholic pop, some nice New Order. I win, and we discover that when men peer into a car that is blasting "True Faith" on the outskirts of San Francisco, they are disappointed to see three women. Teeter is in the back with SB's dog, Buzzo, who is wearing a neckerchief and a glower.

SB and Teeter come up with a game where you replace the last word of a film title with the word "penis."

The Thin Red Penis

My Own Private Penis

Revolutionary Penis

When we get to the hotel, I take a bath whilst simultaneously washing my bra, T-shirt, and knickers, because they got sweaty from the drive and since I have to hand wash them and hand wash myself I figure it's best to do it at the same time.

SB walks in to use the toilet. "That's some Emma-logic."

"What do you mean?"

"You are dirty and your clothes are dirty and you are together in a bath stewing in your own dirt."

"Oh. I didn't think of that."

Mum, having landed, calls me from the hotel corridor. "I'm lost." Both of us Capricorns, she insists that I am a mountain-climbing goat, whereas she is a yard-dwelling goat.

I notice, during this trip, the ways in which she finally does seem like a seventy-year-old. She is having a hard time putting on seat belts, working ATMs, zipping her own jacket.

SB and Teeter go off to have fun, and Mum and I stay in the hotel room playing with my tarot cards. Over and over again, she keeps drawing "Twin Flame."

That's you and Dad, I say, suddenly churlish that they should have found true love, even if it resulted in my existence.

"Look. I've never told anyone this. I moved to England chasing another man. He never got in touch. I met your father the first week."

I know she was planning to abort me and Dad said, "Let's just take a chance," and they did, they took the chance and they're together over thirty years later.

We are sharing a bed in the dockside room, though I spend most of the night awake, filling in the forms Dr. K has sent over in advance of our meeting. Around 1 a.m., Mum, fast asleep, sits bolt upright and inexplicably announces: "I think I'm going to say 'ooooh.'"

She waits a comedienne's beat (a comedienne's beat, even in her sleep!) and then she says "OOOOOOOH." She instantly turns back over and starts snoring.

"Room service?" says a voice at the door the next morning, and Mum answers by singing, in the manner of Holly Golightly: "Rooom service wiiiider than a mile . . ."

We take a cab, get to Dr. K's early, faff about pretending we might buy clothes at a next-door boutique, when we will not buy clothes at a next-door boutique. In his waiting room, he has the same *New Yorker*s as Dr. R had a year ago. I wonder if he was bequeathed them. Dr. K's office is larger than Dr. R's, with better air breezing through the large window. His chairs are a bit less comfortable, though his air is comforting.

A slight, gray-haired man around the same age as Dr. R, he smiles and goes through the forms I'd filled out in advance. "Huh," he says, behind his desk, "huh."

He looks up. "You are lighting up across the board."

"So I figured out, from these questions, that I'm not a germaphobe or a hypochondriac and I'm not obsessive-compulsive. But all the other answers. What do they say about me?"

"They're indicative of post-traumatic stress disorder."

"Ha. That's brilliant. Love is a battlefield."

He raises his eyebrows, and without his asking, I start to explain myself. When, having eaten up most of the session, I finally stop talking, his response is as straight an answer as one could ever hope to get from a psychiatrist.

"I would advise that you have no contact for at least six months. Don't respond to him, ever. Don't be in touch. Six months."

"Right," I say, "so, OK. But, what happened?"

"What happened? With him?"

He tilts his head upwards as if balancing the answer to my question on the end of his nose.

"Well. There is a psychiatric occurrence we see in men—not often women—where they put all their hopes and dreams onto one person, so intensely that at some point it trips a wire in the brain circuitry, and that causes them to go, in a minute, 180 degrees the other way. That's why it doesn't surprise me that it happened on the plane."

"Do they . . . do they come back from it?"

He has a very sweet smile. "That is not a pattern we've observed before."

"Oh. That makes sense."

"He's a very good actor," he says, and, I answer, "Thanks."

"But great actors," he explains, "are trained to follow their instincts. Great humans are supposed to take instinct and consider and not act on them."

I don't know why I can't say this out loud (I'd have said it to Dr. R), why I say it only in my head:

What people don't understand when you've already been a suicide and pulled through is that after the sadness comes fear: Where is my mind going with this? I don't want to die. I do not want to die. But I've taken the red pill and now I don't know what's going to happen. When you don't have so much control over your own thoughts, over the myriad voices in your head, you don't know where they could go.

What I say is, "I realize, of course, that GH owes me nothing, because that would imply that the world is fair. Dr. R's death proves otherwise."

Dr. K weeps a little, discreetly. Then he gets out a prescription pad.

"I'm going to double your Strattera and add Klonopin, for use as needed."

Watching him write, it occurs to me: "So, how did you know Dr. R?"

"Oh." He looks at me. "I was next door."

"Next door where?"

"The room next door. At East Ninety-fourth Street."

I am stunned.

"I'm really sorry. I never noticed you."

He smiles. "I always wondered what was going on inside that room. I am very glad to meet you, because you came from behind his door."

After the session, Mum takes me to see the Richard Avedon exhibit. Alongside the portraits is a quote from Avedon: "We all perform. It's what we do for each other all the time, deliberately or unintentionally. It's a way of telling about ourselves in the hope of being recognized as what we'd like to be."

I stop at his photo of Janis, fists up, when she still had fight in her. And at Marilyn, in sequins, exhausted. We stand, for a long time, in front of no. 40, Groucho Marx, without makeup, and in old age. Mum says it is who he really is. I ask her why. "There is great depth, and sorrow and dignity." It costs $45,000. I want it. The picture, but also the attributes.

We go to City Lights, the bookstore launched by Lawrence Ferlinghetti, who first published Allen Ginsberg's *Howl*. It's heaven. I buy GH books that I will put under my bed and never give him, but they are there, for him, covered in dust and cat hair, dusted with my snores. One day, they will hear me make love to other men. But they are his. I buy some too for Dr. R. They are in my desk drawer, under my computer. City Lights has every book ever. It fills me with an addict-like need, like I want to fall to my knees and snort them, instead of reading them.

Mum and I are on the tram back to the hotel when I turn on my BlackBerry. An e-mail from GH, a week late, in response to one I'd sent. He says how happy he is. He says how happy I sound. I hand Mum the BlackBerry. She shakes her head. "It is dutiful and—I don't know—weary. It's like he has emotional amnesia."

"I'm on his video card," I blurt, like when someone couldn't have done a murder in the Bronx because their subway card registered a fare to Brooklyn.

She hands me back the BlackBerry.

"I think you have to accept that the GH you knew isn't there at the moment. I was witness to how much he loved you. I have the photos. I have the letters he sent me about you. I have the poems. This isn't the GH I knew. I don't recognize this person. Emma—he's shed his skin."

Her heart is broken too. She has to say the thing that will give me back my life. She draws on every reserve. I see how much it hurts her and it hurts me too. I came from her joy and her pain, I lived in it and I live in it now.

I watch in disbelief as we pass a street with his surname, and one block later a street with the pet name he gave to me. We intersect. He says he thanks every star that we existed on the same celestial plain. But here we are on earth, dirty, well used, a man-made throughway for intersecting dreams.

I say something about Dr. R, about his sudden death. Mum whips her head around.

"GH died? What?!"

"Dr. R!"

"I'm sorry, I was thinking about GH." She pauses. Her face lights up. "I just realized that I want to kill GH."

She puts a miniature Snickers in her mouth.

I look out the window. This is a beautiful city and I had a good time. I thought I would never, ever be back. I thought I could never speak this city's name again, let alone permit it to speak mine. Time heals all wounds. And if it doesn't, you name them something other than wounds and agree to let them stay.

CHAPTER 36

I FORCE MUM TO COME to Shabbat services with me that week. I want her to hear Rabbi Wolpe's sermon. This turns out to be a potent one.

"*So there's a Chassidic story of Rabbi Bunim of Pshischa, who was a famous Chassidic master who was walking with some of his students one day, and he pointed to a bunch of Chassidim and he said, 'You see those Chassidim over there? They're dead.' And the students said, 'What do you mean that they're dead?' and he said, 'They're dead,' and they asked him, 'How do you know they're dead? They're up, they're walking!' and he said, 'Because they've stopped asking questions.' They walked on for a little while and one of his students said to him, 'Rabbi, how do we know we're not dead?' and he said, 'Because you asked.'*"

I look over at Mum.

"*So I want to say something about the asking of questions because I asked myself a brand-new question, not about life, although it turned into that . . . But I was reading the Torah portion this week and it was of course the same Torah portion that occurs each year at this time and I've read it I don't know how many times but I never ask myself the question. It's the part where Jacob wrestles with an angel, and as he wrestles with the angel when the dawn is about to break he says, 'I won't let you go until you bless . . . until you bless me.' And the angel says to him, 'No longer will your name be Jacob but from now your name will be Israel because you have fought with human beings and with angels and survived.' Now I've read that story a lot of times but only this week did it occur to me that he doesn't bless him!"*

Mum is screwing up her face the way she does when she's thinking.

"He doesn't say, 'May you have children, may you have wealth, may you be healthy, may you be happy,' and yet Jacob lets him go! So I knew as is inevitably the case for a good question there must be some answer that speaks to us, to our hearts, to our souls, that means something, why does Jacob let the angel go?"

Here's where I start weeping. Mum looks up at me and I try flicking away the tears with an index finger at each eye.

"And I realized that for Jacob that there must have been a blessing in that, and there was and there is for us. What the angel gave Jacob was the blessing of self-transformation. You don't have to be Jacob anymore. You've struggled. And now you can change."

My tears are now projectile (it's actually quite biblical).

"It doesn't mean that bits of Jacob won't cling to you, they will throughout your life, but they are now subsumed into something greater . . . and he gave him, in fact, the most important blessing— the blessing from which all other blessings flow—which is he gave him the blessing of transforming his soul into something better, something more beautiful, something closer to God, something closer to what he was meant to be . . ."

Unable to draw breath, I wait for oxygen masks to drop from the synagogue ceiling.

"... which is why the next day Jacob can go out and meet Esau, his twin, and make peace. When I read that, I realized how enormously important and also in some ways countercultural it was. You can't open a magazine or read a newspaper without learning how determined you are by your genes, by your environment, by your peers, by your parents, all of us are overprogrammed by all sorts of factors that leave out the possibility that you can transform yourself. Now if you say, well, Jacob, sure he transformed himself but he had the advantage of an angel, I will remind you what the Bible says: Jacob was left alone ... and a man wrestled with him until the coming of the dawn. So if Jacob was alone who wrestled with him? You want to call it an angel? That's OK but it sounds to me closer to the angels of our better nature of Lincoln than an angel with wings. In other words, it was a struggle with himself. And the product of that struggle: anger, bitterness, resentment, envy or transformation, aspiration, hope, decency ... the product of that struggle is the quality of your life and the nature of your soul."

I've just given over to tears now, like it's a new fabric I've invented and will model for the rest of my life.

"That characterizes what we can loosely call a religious worldview, it is the antideterminist worldview, it is the belief that although lots about this world is given, ultimately what's not given is the disposition of your soul toward what you have and what you lack. You know we're about to enter a time where people are going to talk a lot about what they lack, what they don't have, what they once have that was taken away from them and that's a painful thing ... but it's also an opportunity. You can't have an attitude *toward loss if you haven't lost, and you can't know what you really believe about the material goods of this world as long as you are stuffed full of them. This is, if you will, a terrible time for many people, and like all terrible times—a spiritual opportunity. If you are sitting in this congregation, I've said it before and will no doubt say it again, if you're sitting in this congregation you are among the ninety-nine point something percent of the luckiest people who ever lived. Even if your 401k is in the toilet, you still are."*

The thirty-one flavors of pain.

"And the attitude you take toward your good fortune, that's what determines the level of light in your soul. There's no one here who's lost so much that they can't give. No one. And not only that but there's no one here whose soul won't be ennobled by that giving, which is part of the step of self-transformation.

"You know on Hanukah you put the Hanukia, the Hanukah menorah, where? In the window. Because our tradition tells us you must practice 'pirsumei nisa,' which means advertising the miracle, and there are at least two ways of understanding that. One is that you're advertising a miracle that happened a thousand years ago in a temple that no longer exists, that God who is the creator of the universe managed to make oil last for several nights, which frankly, on the scale of God's wonders, you know, once you've created the world, making oil last is not really . . . it's like a creative housewife, you know? All she's got is Hamburger Helper, it's gonna last her all week long, even though if you or I cooked it, we'd get one meal out of it. But there's another miracle, which is that thousands of years ago the temple was destroyed, which meant that the people who lived in the temple dwelt in darkness, and yet here we are in 2008 putting a Hanukia in our windows. The book of Proverbs says that the soul of

a human being is God's candle. It's all about transforming yourself, renewing your light, and knowing that if your light shines it doesn't only shine for you, that you really can make a difference in the world, that you put the Hanukia in the window so other people can see the light. I hope that in the season that comes, however dark it is, you will be a light and share that light. Shabbat Shalom."

CHAPTER 37

———

I GO DOWN TO THE COUNTRY STORE and buy coffee for the first time in a while. Spike immediately says, "How's GH?" I draw a breath.

"He's good."

"That guy is so in love with you. Lilly and I have been together twenty years and we were saying you rarely see energy like that between two people."

I clear my throat. I tell him the truth.

Mum and I do the storied House of Blues Gospel Brunch. From shrimp jambalaya to chocolate banana bread pudding, we eat everything. The gospel singer onstage today beams. "There ain't no party like a Holy Ghost party!" We totally believe her.

Her name is Sunshine and she has very long nails that curl, and she flicks them when she sings "This Little Light of Mine."

You don't even understand how much my mother and I danced that morning. We danced our asses off. On the way out, Mum stops to wrap and put apple fritters in her hand-bag. "*Don't* take an old Jewish lady to a buffet!" she snaps, when I roll my eyes.

That evening, we watch *Slumdog Millionaire*, which is getting raves. When the credits roll, Mum turns to me, takes off her glasses, and says, evenly: "You have caused me to watch a film about poo."

When we wake up, we play tarot, as has become habit. Mum pulls, from the deck, a card with a baroque painting of a blond man holding out a golden bowl. She looks at it. "I would hate it if I went downstairs and instead of there being coffee, there was that guy saying, 'I got you this bowl.'"

She makes me laugh harder than anyone I've ever known. And then the next thing she says is:

"I woke up feeling so sad that you cry so much."

She doesn't have her contact lenses in yet, so she's wearing glasses that make her look like a tiny vole.

"It's OK, Mum. I'm used to it."

After she's left, I make the decision that I can't keep traveling to San Francisco, so I go to see a psychiatrist in Beverly Hills, suggested by Dr. K. I am angry about going. I don't even write down his name, just his suite number. The waiting room looks like a brain. He, himself, looks like all those times when Jim Carrey plays a serious role and never gets an Oscar.

I tell him, straightaway, about losing Dr. R, and how I only found out something was up by calling to make an appointment and getting a message saying the office was closed. And that's all I knew, until I opened the e-mail from his brother-in-law saying he had died.

"That's terrible. That's *not* OK!"

I'm shocked. It sounds like he's angry at a dog.

I have become used to defending GH; now I'm defending Dr. R.

"Well, aren't people allowed to die how they want to die? Even if it means leaving their patients in the dark?"

He disagrees most vehemently.

Then I tell him about GH.

"That is appalling!"

I hope, suddenly, that he is easily appalled. I've been crying for two months now but all of a sudden I desperately do not want to be right. I want him to say I've been having inappropriate reactions. Because I'm crazy. Maybe I'm sick. Maybe my meds are off.

I tell him about the Baskin-Robbins thirty-one flavors of pain and that what I'm going through is really OK in the scheme of things.

"It's just that we made so many plans and he kept pushing them. The places we were going to go, the children we were going to have."

"Of course you were making plans. Of course. If you were seventeen. If you were twenty-two, I'd have said "slow down." Not at thirty-two. That's why it hurts so much. Because the plans were appropriate."

I think about Dr. R's plans with Barbara.

"Well then, I don't know if it was real, and that makes me feel like I'm going insane again."

"Absolutely it was real. It was a real, *partial* picture. Because it ended preemptively, things you would have learned about him in the relationship, you are instead learning in the breakup. You have learned that he has a desperate desire for intimacy and then a desperate desire for the cave. He will get lonely there eventually and come back."

"To me?"

He doesn't pause. "To someone new."

"And I'll have to watch another girl?"

"You will have to be Cassandra and know what lies ahead for that girl."

I ask if I can show him a picture of us together. It occurs to me that this doctor, who treats crazy people, has never met me, he knows nothing, he could think I made it all up.

He looks through the photos. "You look extremely happy."

I frown. "We were."

As I take back the photos I say: "I just want them both to explain it to me. I want to know how two people I loved, so much, died without me ever knowing they were sick."

He folds his hands across his knees.

"You absolutely deserve an explanation and you absolutely will not get one."

After the session, I stop in a department store to buy red lipstick I don't need—all red lipstick is red lipstick, no red lipstick is needed. The man behind the NARS counter puts it on me. He has dark skin, light hair, and light eyes; he kind of reminds me of Christopher when I met him, but super gay. He tries to match the shade to my skin tone but he's having trouble. "It's hard to tell what suits me at the moment because I've been crying a lot."

"A man?"

I nod.

He waves his lipstick brush in my face. "No more of that."

I wave goodbye to him and skip out into the street, leaning towards mania, most likely, and I dance at the stop sign and I walk and walk as one is not intended to do in Los Angeles. I realize: I am frightening people. It is such a blessing not to feel frightened.

I understand that from the night GH and I met, he was already saying goodbye. I understand that though Dr. R did not prepare me for his death, he was preparing me for the end from the first session. The difference is, I showed up to meet Dr. R bleeding, but I showed up to meet GH healed.

CHAPTER 38

_____

I AGREE TO A BLIND DATE with a nice Jewish boy. As soon as we meet, he says: "I know your story. I hope you don't mind me saying that." He picks me up, takes me to the movies, takes me to dinner, insists on paying for everything. When he kisses me, I cry. I explain it's not because I wish he were someone else, it's because it's such a shock to the system to be desired after feeling so completely abandoned.

We watch *The Picture of Dorian Gray*, with Angela Lansbury. In the film, Dorian worships her and then she sleeps with him and after that, he writes her a letter saying she will never be a part of his life again. When she gets the letter, she kills herself.

The man I'm watching with is a cantor—he's a fucking cantor—it's absurd. But it's no more or less absurd than a movie star. They both work in the realm of projected dreams. The menorah, like true cinema, is an object purely of beauty. It is not functional. It is there only to be admired. Even the Shabbat lights you can read by. I think of GH. I say a prayer for him and let the cantor drive me home.

In the car, he plays the White Stripes' cover of Bob Dylan's "One More Cup of Coffee." He plays a cover of my Gypsy Husband's song that totally rearranges it.

He isn't the one. But he is kind to me.

When I get home, I start trying to figure out a way to get back my suicide letter from GH. Is it a letter or a note? It's only eight lines. Novella or even a short story, except it doesn't have a beginning, middle, and end, it's a suicide mission statement.

I took back my dresses off his hangers, my shoes from his closet, my underwear from his drawers. I didn't get back my Magimix, my cake stand, my Star of David necklace. I don't want to take back any of the poems I wrote him, but I would take back all the poems he wrote about me. I wish we hadn't prayed together, on our knees, in my garden at 7 a.m. I'd like never to have met him, because he made me so happy.

Mum says a thing that upsets me terribly, and we don't speak for a few days. What she says when she calls is: "I saw a play about GH last night." Her voice sounds strained and raw.

"What was the play?"

She takes a breath. "*Hamlet.*"

I'm silent.

She adds, "I've never wept at *Hamlet* before."

I still write to him every few weeks: notes that are not even passive-aggressive, they're just bizarre and random, about what I'm having for dinner and what I've just seen at the movies. I get him a subscription to the Sunday paper. I'll show you the error of your ways! By arranging for you to receive free delivery of the *New York Times*. There can be a very thin line between heartbreak and performance art.

GH will never, ever answer my texts. There is a greater possibility that Dr. R will reply. But I still send them. My cats come to me because I feed them. It's in their hotwire—I've spoiled them for so long. If I suddenly stopped leaving them food, they would still come to me for it.

Sometimes I feel the texts I send are like leaving prayers at the Wailing Wall. If Dr. R can't hear me, and GH is deaf too, maybe G-d can? I have so much hope—these are the words that will stir him back to life, G-d or Dr. R or GH. I have so much hope. Until I hit Send. And then I have no faith at all.

At the end of the week, Mum sends me a lovely letter from London.

Emma. It will get better now. You can allow the whole thing to recede. You've had your movie star. He's had his smart, funny, sensitive girl from something like the real world. You'll find someone more grounded. He'll find someone tougher. Done.

Reading that letter, I move the loss of GH and the death of Dr. R from being a picture in my wallet I see all through the day to going in a photo album to be looked at on special occasions.

MAY 17, 2008

*I'll always keep the image of my beloved oldest brother,
windsurfing across the horizon toward Gardiners Island.
Balanced, athletic, gliding effortlessly between surf and sky.
Coming in from the water, you begin to see the big smile, the
charisma that lights us all up as he looks at you and connects.
He made the world a better place, a happier, more secure
place. He brought us together with warmth, humor, and optimism. He helped a lot of people, patients and otherwise, by
lending his humanity, and leaving no doubt that they were
understood.*

   *He was devoted to Sam and Andy. Not all of us are
blessed with long life, but his boys are his legacy and he was
so proud of them. He fought like hell to the very end to have
more time with his family.*

A (POTOMAC FALLS, VA)

CHAPTER 39

—————————

I START TALKING TO another devoted patient of Dr. R's. We find each other on Facebook and, after sharing loving memories, eventually I confess to the part of me that is angry at him for not warning us he was dying. And angry that I still don't know what happened. He was there for me completely. And then he was gone, with only a confusing voice message to untangle it. I couldn't bring myself to probe Barbara for the details. My new Facebook friend suggests I speak to Dorothy Rick, a psychiatric colleague of Dr. R's.

Dorothy agrees to talk to me, and I fly back to New York to see her. Her office is large and beautiful. She is beautiful and tiny. She looks like a precocious little girl as she curls into her leather chair. And I ask her, why, why, didn't he give me any warning?

"Because the level of denial was profound. I saw him in the hospital a week before he died . . ."

"Which hospital?"

"Columbia." She hands me a preemptive tissue. "He was

sitting up, but very weak. It had been grueling and Barbara needed a break, but no one believed this was the end."

I screw up the tissue without using it.

"When was he diagnosed, exactly?"

"August 2007. He called me and said, 'There's news that's not good, but I'm going to beat it.' It was stage three."

"Meaning?"

"It was in both lungs."

"Was he a smoker?"

"No. He was hoping to have surgery, with chemo and radiation, shrinking the tumor so that they could operate. And they did do that."

"When?"

"February. They were very, very hopeful. They believed chemo had taken care of it and he was doing very well post-op, he was in great spirits."

She pushes her hair back from her face. I am glad. I want to see everything.

"A month after surgery, they did a CAT scan and found something and it was not good news. But he was seeing a top oncologist who was telling him we can try this protocol."

"What's that?"

"Atypical treatments. He had to be hospitalized to do that. And that's when he got pneumonia. He was still practicing two weeks before he was hospitalized."

That's when I used up a whole session telling him about stupid HEWZ VAN and the fucking Abba-Zabas. Whilst he struggled to keep his breathing even, I was nattering on about nothing, because I didn't really need him that day.

"Emma, we spoke and he sounded weak and he was very

sick, but very hopeful. And that was the truth. He specifically asked me not to tell the patients we shared."

"So he died of . . . ?"

"He died of pneumonia. Barbara said he wasn't supposed to die. The kind of cell he had was curable." She sighs. "He didn't believe he was dying, so he was being honest. I'm telling you now: he didn't betray you."

Then I cry. I uncrumple the tissue. She waits for me to get it together, until I ask her, how exactly, she would define Dr. R's method of psychiatry.

"He was into harm reduction. That's new thinking of the last five to ten years, and it's how you keep people coming back. Old-school psychiatry is about being a 'tabula rasa,' which means blank screen. But psychiatry has evolved since then. We all started doing training at the same time and realized that wall was over. Humanity is key. As Dr. R proved, you're most effective when you're a mensch."

Then she asks me to tell her a little bit about myself, to tell her what's been going on. I tell, for the fiftieth time, the story of GH and his 180, and how hard I've been working to understand it.

"You're not gonna find an answer. There isn't one. The answer's you. The answer is, despite it all, you're not hurting yourself anymore."

She's very good. She sounds a lot, in her thinking, like *him*.

I ask her, "What would Dr. R say?"

She grins.

"Well, let me put on my Dr. R hat."

"What does a Dr. R hat look like?"

Is it a baseball hat? Was it there the whole time and it was just another one of the things I wasn't looking at about him because I didn't know what would happen next? Did it say Yankees or Mets? (Note to self: ask Barbara if he supported the Yankees or the Mets.)

Dorothy puts up her hand. "It looks like common sense. He'd say walk away."

I want to say, "How?" In what manner would he want me to walk away? When I was at school "Mysterious Ways" by U2 was a huge hit and I'd invent mysterious ways in which to move (I'd ask to be excused from chemistry for the toilet and walk to the bathroom mysteriously). How might he want me to leave GH?

It's like she can see it all swirling under my skin.

"Look. I get it: you're a writer and he's a great psychological profile, but I don't know how much good that's gonna do you, honestly."

"Do you believe he meant it all the times he said we were going to be a family?"

"I believe *he believed* everything he said to you."

Then she shakes her head and says a very strange thing.

"It's just a movie."

"What?"

"It's not real. You don't have to feel as hurt as you do. It was only a movie."

I love this woman. I ask if I can see her again when I'm next in New York. We agree to make it a regular appointment when I stop through.

On the way out the door, I remember to ask her how and where she met Dr. R.

"Oh," she says, "I trained him."

CHAPTER 40

IN DECEMBER I SPEND CHRISTMAS and my birthday in Istanbul, just as GH had planned. But I go without him. As I navigate the amorphous abstraction of disappointment, it is a thrill to be somewhere that is full of "Yes" and "No" answers. The "Yes" and "No" of Islam. The call to prayer that blares across the city every morning. Then the dance music that keeps you up at night. The architecture, full of squares, cubes, and spheres. My favorite is the Aya Sofya—the Byzantine church with its four added minarets.

Staying in a cheap hotel where each room, instead of being numbered, is named for a Turkish love poem, I eat baklava every evening, and drink tiny coffees.

I feel so much more courage in Istanbul.

My bed is single and my room spartan, but I can admire the Sea of Marmara from my window. Silhouettes dance across the moonlight: on top of the horizontal line of the Marmara there is a continuous horizontal band of city walls, red roofs and mosques rising up pale between them. It could have been sad being here, this trip he had fantasized. But it isn't.

Le Corbusier said, "Everything leads me to single out the Turks. They were polite, solemn, they had respect for the presence of things. Their work is huge and beautiful and grandiose."

It is just the city in which to harbor enormous feelings. In California, I felt that the expanse of nature outside my house—the vast sky, the mountains, the endless trees— was surely helping me pull through. But there's something about this city with its man-made grandiosity that I find soothing, anchoring. Anything can be achieved. Everything is within my power.

Walking the streets, there are stray cats everywhere, sad-eyed, seeking shelter from the rain. They look like hopped-up Edie Sedgwick in disheveled calico fur. There is no cat food at the nearest deli, so I buy salami, have them chop it up, and spend my birthday feeding the cats. I understand I am a psychopath to care more about animals than humans, but there are no homeless humans here, or dogs. Just home-less cats.

It is soon snowing mercilessly. On Friday, I light Shabbat candles in my little hotel room. Turkey remains the only truly moderate Islamic country, and they are deeply proud of it. I leave behind the irrationality of the last few months, and it is a joy to be in a place where people are constitution-ally reasonable, when all the countries around them are half mad.

I visit the Blue Mosque, the last great mosque of the classical period, incorporating Byzantine elements with traditional Islamic architecture, its interior adorned with blue tiles. My hair is very dark and long now, and as the snowstorm whips it in circles around my face, the mosque lends a faint tint of blue to my skin. I take out my compact mirror, vanity in the long shadow of devotion. The looking glass tells a story of a girl who lives under the sea.

Jet-lagged, I treat myself to a 6 a.m. breakfast at the Four Seasons. I eat pastries and read the Turkish paper. On my way out, I steal food for the cats. It isn't stealing because I paid fifty dollars for a buffet, but I enjoy experiencing it as a transgression. Salmon, sausages, and bacon galore, for the non-halal felines.

Morning just breaking, I walk over to Cemberlitas Hamam, the oldest Turkish bath in the city. It was built in 1584 and the only light comes from the hundreds of stars cut out of the domed roof. I can hear the call to prayer from the Blue Mosque as I lie, naked, in the piping-hot steam. There is no one else there.

Each female visitor to the hammam is assigned a woman to scrub and clean them, to beat and knead their aching limbs. The women who scrub you are, themselves, naked. My woman has enormous, pendulous breasts and the pale gray eyes I'm used to seeing in New York on Dominicans. As we try our best to communicate, she lathers my hair, laughing and saying to me: "Baby girl."

I cannot tell if she is saying I *look* like I am a baby girl, or asking if I have a baby girl.

She grins. She is missing a tooth. "Baby girl."

She says it again, beaming. "Baby girl?"

I have a terrible moment, where I decide she must be asking about Pearl. Enveloped in steam, tears prick my eyes. I am glad when soap fills them.

At the exit, they sell home-made soap with the evil eye attached, to protect yourself from people who'd wish you ill. I buy one, wondering, How do you hang it inside yourself?

The nineteenth-century French adventurer Pierre Loti wrote *Aziyadé*, about the Istanbul harem girl he fell in love with. He said he had found his soulmate. They planned to escape the harem and make a life together. And then, one morning, his ship sailed home, with him on it. When he returned, many years later, he found that *Aziyadé* had died of love for him. The book doesn't say she killed herself. It says she died of love. I suppose she stopped eating. Maybe her heart really did break beneath her jeweled veil.

"Are you mine?"

Yes.

"Are you mine?"

Yes.

"Are you mine?"

No.

"No?"

No. I loved being yours. But now I'm mine, which is all I ever was, in the end.

Dodging snowstorms, I wander to Topkapi Palace, which from 1465 to 1863 was home to the Ottoman sultans. A complex of four main courtyards and many intricate smaller buildings, it has hundreds of rooms and chambers, containing the most holy relics of the Muslim world, as well as the well-preserved harem rooms.

When I visit, the exhibition running is called The Sacred Trusts. They are displaying the cooking vessel of the Prophet Abraham, the turban of the Prophet Joseph, the Prophet David's sword, the Prophet Muhammad's cloak. I find the guidebook especially compelling:

> The past, future, and present are each various dimensions of a single unity. We are able to relish this unity as we sense these various depths of time—one being essential, the others secondary and intertwined. There are some objects, however, which are like a point or a line drawn, connecting us with our spiritual roots. Through the associations they conjure, we can delve more profoundly into the past and we can cherish hopeful expectations for the future, armed with a persistence, endurance, and determination that are necessary for the time to come.

I spend hours there, until I find myself separated from the crowd, in an unexpected side room that I can't find noted in the guidebook. Beneath the elaborate gold-leaf calligraphy, there is a sofa, a fan, and a small coffee table bearing old issues of *The New Yorker*.

A door opens.

"Em-ma For-rest!"

"Dr. R?" So this is where he's been. "Can I hug you?"

He nods.

"Michelle's a hugger. You know? Michelle Obama. You missed that. But she loves to hug people."

"These are different times."

"Yeah."

He leads me into his office and settles in his chair.

"Can you turn off that light?"

"Right, of course, and that one."

"Thank you."

The room is just as it has always been, and the schoolkids of East 94th Street can be heard rattling by on their bikes.

"So . . ." He smiles. Opens his hands towards me, which I know means, "Where's your head at?"

"I've been having a hard time without you."

He nods. "Bereavement is hard. You've been very lucky. You haven't lost anyone before. Your reaction is not inappropriate. All those years of cutting. Now you have a reason to be in pain. It's an interesting challenge."

"Thank you!"

"I have no question that you're up to it. You're completely different from the girl who was on my doorstep."

"Do you think you could have helped him?"

He shifts. He knows who I am talking about. "Yes."

I drop my head.

"But this isn't your concern."

"Do you think he meant the things he said?"

"I do. He meant everything he said, when he said it. But this is his default. And it won out. Right now you're depressed about one thing. Before you were depressed about everything. These are good times for you, Emma."

I look at the ground, I look up with wet eyes.

"I'm afraid of loving again. I'm afraid I've lost my faith."

"You haven't."

"The trapdoor I have in my mind? That can go to those bad places? It almost gave way again."

"You know the ways to keep it nailed shut."

I shake my head. "Because of you, I'm even more afraid of my mum dying. I'm mourning her now. I'm trying to inoculate myself."

"It won't help when it happens."

I am afraid to remind him of this . . .

"I told you in our last face-to-face that I had started to obsess about you dying."

He smiles. "The point of psychiatry is that it should be terminated." I flinch but he continues. "We don't want you to be with us forever. I want to get you out of here. I want us to figure out how you can grieve this and let go."

I search for something good to say, something to tell him he's right to trust in me.

"I'm glad I came to Istanbul. I really am. But even though I'm glad I did this, I still believe that you truly find yourself not in travel, but in other human souls."

"Then you're still the woman I knew."

"I was a kid when we first met."

I cover my eyes with a tissue, like a fan, like the silly fan GH once sent me from Spain.

"Let me tell you something, and I want you to remember it: who you authentically are—there is no one and nothing that can add to or subtract from that."

"But . . . in the closet that afternoon, in the bathtub, I thought: I've lost so much. I should just lose it all."

"You know you don't have to. It's like the story you told me about drawing on your face when you were a kid. About deliberately failing the math test because you were afraid of failing the math test. You can break that pattern."

"When he came in me, he'd weep. You know? You know? In hindsight, it makes me feel like I was a sin eater."

"Emma. Emma. You are not a sin eater. You got on the wrong train. That's all."

I put the tissue fan down, all my cards on the table, wet, all stuck together.

"I miss you. That's what I meant to tell you. I really just miss you, terribly, terribly, terribly. And goodness doesn't get to stay. It just doesn't get to stay. The longest I've ever known it to stay . . . is my parents."

Dr. R scratches out a note on his pad.

"Losing you both was only the practice pain, wasn't it? For my mum and dad . . ."

He puts his finger on his lips, his elbow at his chest, not racked with cancer. "Yes."

"And when that happens, this will seem like nothing."

He nods.

"When it happens," he asks me, "what will get you through?"

"Friends who love me."

"And if your friends weren't there?"

"Music through headphones."

"And if the music stopped?"

"A sermon by Rabbi Wolpe."

"If there was no religion?"

"The mountains and the sky."

"If you leave California?"

"Numbered streets to keep me walking."

"If New York falls into the ocean?"

Your voice in my head.

At the Istanbul outpost of his office, leaving my psychiatrist for the very last time, I sign Dr. R's check and hope it will not bounce. But I know that if it does, he will forgive me.

CHAPTER 41

TO GET HOME, I have to change in London. There's a layover, so I go into town and find myself, almost to my own bewilderment, walking into the Tate.

My heart is pumping as I get to room fourteen.

There are other girls, gawping, seeing her for the first time. I hang back, let them have their moment with her. I wait my turn.

The first night I spend back in L.A., there is, at 3 a.m., a clatter at the front door. The cats' hair stands on end. I reach for the nearest thing to use as a weapon. Under my pillow there is . . . a pen. I will write them away. Nothing happens. Whoever is trying to burgle the place, they can't get in. They are felled by the lock GH had installed in my home to protect me. But the funny thing is, it reminds me how often I do reach for the pen lately. Anytime I want to die, I write a story instead.

I get out of bed, go down to the computer, and start writing a screenplay that I will write for three days straight, a comedy called *Liars* (*A–E*). It sells to the Oscar-winning producer Scott Rudin, for more money than I have ever seen. I pay off my tax. I pay off my debts. I pay back everyone I owe, realizing, as I do, that the loan I'm returning to my dad dates all the way back to the Priory.

The day after the inauguration, my dad spends an inordinate amount of time Photoshopping Aretha Franklin's hat onto my baby photos.

Malia and Sasha take photos of their daddy, as if there might not be any. Barack memorizes an exquisite seventeen-minute speech and then the swearing in is a mess. Such is life.

MAY 8, 2008

Dr. R helped me catch my first, and only, fish.

E (NEW YORK, NY)

CHAPTER 42

─────────────

I DON'T EXERCISE EVERY DAY and I don't meditate every day, but I do think of suicide every day, as if nodding respectfully at it on my way to work. Some days I awake with the thought of it, or am woken by it. Other days it comes to me when I don't get out of bed fast enough. More rarely, it is my last thought as I drift to sleep. I haven't ever had the thoughts once I am out in the world. It isn't often reactive—it's unusual that something happens to make me think, I should kill myself! It's something softer, something more like a scent. Is it my signature scent, I've come to wonder, and I barely notice it. Just every few years it gets overpowering. For the most part, the touch of the cats distracts me. Music distracts me. Making love—when I am in love—distracts me.

I wonder if *he* knew—if that's what he was smelling in my hair? A component. A top note. There is one period and one alone when I didn't think of it at all, and that's when I was with him. I wish it weren't true. I hope he simply met me at the fruition of Dr. R's work. It's possible.

Dr. R and GH were, to me, two sides of a coin. They made me feel so good. They made me feel I was a good person. They saw something else. *They saw me.* And now they can't see me at all. It's just sad. It's just sad and that's all it is. Because I can still see them. I can see the world I was in.

You want to know, but are afraid to ask, whether or not I found someone. If there could be anyone to fill that hole in my heart after I lost him.

I did.

"Life is futile," says my new therapist, Michaela, "and no one gets out of it alive. There is only love."

She is as different from Dr. R as could be. But isn't that always the way?

I feel very tied to her. And, yet, I know that even if we were to stay together forever: one of us is going to go first.

The sadness—the general sadness that squats and pees inside my brain—isn't over. It never will be. I know how best to chase it away, though. It usually works. Sometimes it doesn't. One day I sit down on the sidewalk and sob so hard a woman comes up and asks if she can pray with me. I say yes. I will always be grateful to that woman. She was pretty, young, she was wearing the omnipresent Juicy Couture tracksuit. She looked like she had just worked out. She prayed until the bus came and then I went home and made tea and wrote a note to myself:

Fuck it, then. I choose this.
It chooses me. I choose it back.

At Portobello Market I buy a Victorian ring. It has a skull with a snake woven through it, it costs five hundred pounds, the most I've ever spent on one thing except my computer. "Scott Rudin bought me that," I say as I slip it on my finger, though I also say the same thing when I buy cat food and toilet paper. I buy it because I want to be like the girls wed to their virginity by their promise ring. I want to look at it every day and let the idea of death glitter and sparkle and that's it. It stays on my finger. It doesn't usually work out too well for the virgins: there's a lot of blow jobs and arse sex that goes towards preserving sex until marriage. And in a weird way I imagine my preserving death until death to be the same. I will probably make a lot of strange decisions in the name of staying alive. I am OK with that.

I told Dr. R New York brought it all to the surface like the medieval use of leeches to draw fever. My Gypsy Husband was like marrying New York. He was the best city in the world, he was the only city in the world, until he closed in on me.

If killing yourself is not an option anymore, you have to sink into the dark instead, and make something out of it.

Perry slaps me in the face in my sleep. I wake up at 6 a.m. feeling, instead of sadness: anger and the need to pee. Something takes me down to the garden. I find the place where I buried the box of low-fat lasagna. I pull down my pajama bottoms, crouch low, and piss on it. As my eyes drift, I see Perry, slightly to my right, watching me with the intense concentration of a bodyguard.

MAY 7, 2008

Our favorite memory of Dr. R was when we were on line for a lift at Jiminy Peak and we saw a man dressed in only swim trunks outside in below-zero temperatures happily jumping in and out of the nearby hot tub. As we looked closer, we realized it was Dr. R (who we did not even know was there at the time) having the time of his life.

J AND J (NEW YORK, NY)

CHAPTER 43

_____

I'M WRITING A NEW SCREENPLAY at a wooden desk in a Tuscan barn house from the fifteenth century. I'm with a man who was briefly my boyfriend but is now my friend, and he's a dear one, one of the dearest, *even* after I have coerced him into admitting that I am "sexually, just not his thing," and even after I have compiled, in a resulting fit of pique, an outlandish secret list of what "his thing" might be ("Page 3 Girls with six fingers?" "Marmite?" "Voiceover by Morgan Freeman?" "The *Ghostbusters* theme song?" "The theme song from *Ghostbusters 2?*"). We've eaten fresh tomatoes and cheese and then pastry with pine nuts and drunk the best coffee ever. He's downstairs writing at his desk and I'm a floor above in a tower. I decide to listen to "Postcards from Italy" by Beirut. It's an amazing song. I mean, it's a lot of other things too, so much history with GH there. But it's also just a fucking great song. This afternoon, it has no history, just melody and words and it does nothing to my heart but make it expand with the joy I've been feeling all week.

Then my friend comes up the stairs from where he's been working. "Two things: one. Will you read what I've written? And two. Will you stop singing: you sound like a fucking pub singer."

We go into the garden for tea. It's sunny, there's a cat on me, it's sunny, there's a plum tree above me, it's sunny, there's a valley, it's sunny, so I have my glasses on to protect my vision. My friend looks at me and says, "You'll hurt yourself."

"No I won't," and then, "Why?"

"The lenses are different."

"No they're not."

"They are."

I'm getting irritated with him because I don't know what he's on about, and then I take them off and see that I have picked up and have been wearing, for twenty minutes, his glasses, which are not sunglasses but heavy-duty prescription ones.

I replace the glasses with my Ray-Bans, and we speak of it no more.

The cat, tangled and blue-eyed, looks up and says, "Bitch, you has learned nothing."

All is well.

Can I tell you what it's like to live inside Millais' painting of Ophelia? There are patches of water so warm. Drowning, I can see the sky, the branches of trees hanging overhead. It's very beautiful. I will stay afloat for as long as I can. There is a boy who floats alongside me for a while, we hold hands and watch the sky together, feel each other's skin wrinkle and prune because "we're leaning out for love and we will lean that way forever." There is a bend and he drifts away, a current he cannot fight. But there is always the man on the riverbank, the one you can't see, the one under the paint. Like the people who hold out cups to the marathon runners. I can hear him. And he's keeping me afloat. It's so cold and so dark but above me it's open and blue and with the water tugging me down, he's still calling, "Look up! Look up!"

And I do.

I thought I needed to know about my Dr. R's final week, about the diagnosis and the treatment. How did he die? What could have stopped it? But I don't need to know about his death. It is the least important part. What matters to me was his life. I finally accept that not only do I not understand the death of my relationship, but I do not need to. These men were good and kind to me, they loved me and I loved them back and the shock at the finish holds no wisdom. The revelation is not that I lost them but that I had them.

Mum writes me an e-mail about *Synecdoche, New York*. She says she found it very beautiful and very moving. When I ask why, she says, "Because I've been thinking about my own mortality." She's never said this out loud before, we've never acknowledged that she might not live forever.

She trusts me to cope with this information.

I file it away, and feel glad that she's thinking about herself, though thinking about herself means thinking about me. And what I've done to her. And what I'll do without her. And what will become of me.

"I don't need you to be happy with someone," she assures me when I ask if she's disappointed that I haven't yet made love last, "I need you to be happy with yourself."

I had my goodbye with Dr. R. And, truth to tell, I saw GH too, not long after Istanbul, but from as far away as can be. An agency party after a Los Angeles awards show.

I wore a dress I bought when I was with Simon, one Simon had thought too tight, too low-cut. Uncontrollable, overflowing me.

"You will see GH if you go," said Mum.

"I know."

"You are brave."

"I am that. Also . . . I am without skin and without dignity."

In this dress, all the tattoos are visible. They patch me over where my blood would come out. That wasn't how they started, but it's what they became.

At the party, I spend a long time talking to Robert Downey Jr. and I completely forget I ever sent him prison packages. I wonder if he remembers that he was in prison. Our other lives before we were saved, before we were pre-modern.

But what you really want to know about is the conversation with GH. It was basic, really: "How's your mum and dad?" "How are your sisters?"

Until an actress with a slender body the color of fattening truffles comes up and jokingly declares that she is finally ready to fuck him. And he says, "Ha! Finally!" because what can he say? Her hair is expertly colored and back-combed. We are in Hollywood. I have elected to be here and I have elected to be *here*.

He and I continue to make small talk. It is small. It is tiny. It engulfs us like Lilliputians. Then there's a moment when the Lilliputians are distracted by miniature cheeseburgers. We break our ropes and we find ourselves holding hands for a while, saying nothing, for probably five minutes. It is quiet and still, so quiet, it takes the actress a while to see and then she gets on her knees before us and says, "I am so mortified about what I said. You two are obviously together."

"I . . ." I start to explain.

She puts up a hand, her nails pearlescent; our history glows in the dark. "There's obviously something here between you."

Somewhere very far away in the Buddhist field where we lay together, the waves are still crashing. There is another life there, where the love letters were not written in disappearing ink. Another life where Dr. R has an extra year, another five years, a life where he doesn't die, a life where he just keeps healing and healing others, his family gets to keep him. It's quiet in our Buddhist field, both of us, after lives of such self-inflicted tumult, gobsmacked by this thing called peace. We have worked so hard to get well and now we have each other to show for it, here, in the heather, on the edge of a cliff from which we feel no impulse to jump. One more moment, one more breath. But there aren't any more. At New York–Presbyterian, behind a door of the Milstein Pavilion, Dr. R takes his last breaths.

As the industry party comes back into focus, and with it the sound of the heather and the sea replaced by the clink of champagne glasses, stilettos on marble, its own wave, GH lets my hand drop and looks the actress in the eye.

"No, darling. Nothing here. There's absolutely nothing."

When I come to the end of my life—when I come to the real end, at the right time, (even if like Dr. R's it is an unfair time, it will be right)—my mind may flash with random images: pencil sharpeners and penguins. My friends who dotted the highway of despair, my father making up a song for a cat, dancing to gospel music with my mother, her straight spine and soft hands and sweet face. My sister's self-stitched gifts. Listening to *Graceland* on car rides. Creating a universe out of reading in silence with your lover. And a man who, though I never saw him outside one small room, believed that life is vast and worth living. I am not being hopeful about this when I say my last thoughts will be of love. I remember it. If you have ever lost someone the way I tried to go, I can assure you to the best of my experience that as despairing as they were, the hell they were in, whatever caused them to swallow the pills or tie the noose, to fill their pockets with rocks and step into the water, before going under, their final thoughts are of love.

I wake to an e-mail from the love of my life.

> I've been thinking about what happens to female voices as they grow older. Both Emmylou Harris and Joan Baez are shot. Those pure, soaring effortless sounds are gone. Joni Mitchell, however, sounds better an octave lower, as do Dylan and Cohen. Everybody ends up sounding like Tom Waits, sooner or later.
>
> I have Emmylou's new album. Her voice is gone but the dramatic power and musicianship is still there and the songs are lovely.

I am walking the icy streets like a very, very old person, trying not to fall.

xxx Mum

MAY 09, 2008

The sportswriter Red Smith, asked to speak at a friend's funeral, looked out at the assembled mourners and said, "Dying is no big deal; the least of us will manage it. Living is the trick."

Dr. R had the most fun being alive of anyone I have ever known. In the twenty-five years that we were friends, he simply enjoyed life. He liked New York, he liked the Hamptons, he liked Saint Barts, he liked theater and music, food and art, watching sports and doing sports, he liked going out, and he liked staying home. He did not do all of these things well; no one does. But he was completely unself-conscious, and willing to try, and willing to laugh at the things that went badly as well as celebrate the things that worked out.

Reading the notes from his patients, I am reminded that there was a serious side to Dr. R too, and that, for a living, he helped people get their lives together. But for anyone who ever wondered why he was good at that, it was because his own life was together, and he believed that life was good and worth living and that it could get better.

A person like Dr. R can get sick, his body can break, and he can leave us bereft. But the light of his smile and the warmth with which he lived does not die. Those things will sustain us forever.

B (PALO ALTO, CA)

CHAPTER 44

———————

MY PARENTS AND I have taken a trip together, staying with SB and her family at their lake house, in New Hampshire. When we arrive there, the lakes and the trees and the gliding hawks are good enough for my soul. But my favorite thing is how every single license plate bears the New Hampshire state motto: "Live free or die."

And, walking around the lake, with my mum and my dad and SB, it occurs to me for the first time, like the first time it dawned on me that cutting is a bad thing, even if it works:

Alone with a cat in a dusty closet full of mismatched shoes is a poor place to let your little light shine.

Mum lets me slip my arm through hers. She whispers to me:
"You know the director David Gordon Green?"
"Yes," I say.
"You know the actor Joseph Gordon-Levitt?"
"Of course."

"They're different from each other."

She waits for me to rebuff this.

"Yes, Mum. They're different men."

She mulls my response.

"No. Not acceptable."

Dad, striding ahead of us with his John Cleese legs, begins to instigate a rousing round of songs from *West Side Story*.

"'WHEN you're a JET you're a JET all the way from your first cigarette to your LAST DYIN' DAY!'"

Dr. R would love this. He'd love to be on a lake with us, side by side by Sondheim.

Then Dad and I move on to "Jerusalem," the English hymn we always had to sing at school.

"'And was Jerooooooselem BUILDED HERE,'" sings my father, with all his might, "'AMONG these dark satanic mills?'"

"What the hell is that song about?" I ask.

"Oh," he shrugs, "Just general William Blake mentalism." After all they've gone through with me, he is offhand in his description of madness and the power it can hold.

I know I'll always have moments of panic that I might be going crazy. (I watched an hour of Rick Moranis clips on YouTube. I downloaded "Ride Like the Wind" by Christopher Cross. I once ate fifty pecans. By "once" I mean one hour ago. Sometimes, during sex, I fantasize about the scene in *Inglourious Basterds* when Shosanna burns down the room full of Nazis.) But the worries are getting further apart.

Dad and I start singing again. Mum is trailing behind us, because she is one foot tall and her legs are made of candy mice. I'm still doing the Jets choreography, and Dad is reaching the crescendo of "Jerusalem."

I say out loud, "I'm really fucking happy." But nobody can hear me because of Dad bellowing the hymn's final notes: "BA BA BAA BA BUUUUUUH!"

MAY 17, 2008

I am a patient of Dr. R's and I always will be.

N (NEW YORK, NY)

EPILOGUE

_____

IT'S IN NEW YORK, six months after our breakup, that a kindly journalist e-mails me a photo of GH hand in hand with his new Gypsy Wife, wearing a dress that reveals her to be in her second trimester of their pregnancy. I'm not quite sure what I'm supposed to do. I know I'm supposed to cut myself. That's the hotwire.

Here's the sofa they lie on. Here's his hand in her hair. Here's his words on her page. Here's how much he needs her. Here's how he kissed her the first time. Here's how she makes him complete.

I look at the razor in my wash kit. "Tell me what to do." The razor stays silent. "Tell me!" I can hear my own breath. Which is to say: I can hear me. There are no voices. Not him. Not Dr. R. Not the Internet crazies. Not even my mum.

I walk out of the bathroom.

I put on my headphones.

I take the 1 train to the Staten Island Ferry.

I'm riding the ferry because it's something I've never done before. The sky is open and vast, it's crisp but sunny, that NYC blue sky, I'm listening to the Velvet Underground singing "Pale Blue Eyes," and since there's no one in my life who has pale blue eyes, I'll have the sky be my muse for the song's duration. The deck is open. There's no one except me. I dance to the music alone. I'm Gypsy Wife. I'm Jeffrey and Judy's Baby Emma. I'm Lisa's sister. I'm the mother of a six-year-old child. I'm a patient on a psychiatric ward. I'm the girl eating crisps to push down the crisps. I'm the girl in the painting. I'm despairing. I'm elated. I am Jane Eyre—I have rescued him from himself! I have finally set him free!—until there is a new Jane Eyre and I am Mrs. Rochester. I have lived in the house. I have lived in the attic. I am a loose end fashioned from a Gordian knot that cannot be untied. I didn't hang myself. I am not sorry.

There are touches of Israeli folk and some of the belly dancing I learned in Istanbul, a little flamenco in my feet. I dance my ass off, up and down the deck. I can do what I like, because I am alone.

The ferry rounds the corner and the Statue of Liberty makes me want to stand up and cheer—I've always been that way about female beauty; I once saw Debbie Harry in a doctor's waiting room and shouted "Hoorah!"—of course the symbol of liberty and hope is female. A little boy is outraged to hear he can't go inside her. "Look at her? That's it? You don't do anything? You just look?"

Homeless people ride the ferry because it's free; there's a sign that says "Are you bipolar?" and ticks off a list of possible symptoms, and at the top of the stairs, like a high-concept advertising teaser campaign, there's a man who is bipolar or at least very down on his luck, but I'm not afraid.

I think of what Dr. R would have done with him, what he would have seen in him, seen in this. Leaning on the deck, a woman accidentally jabs her arm into me because she is being kissed. Whatever becomes of these lovers, she will always remember this moment, and it may cause pain, maybe for a long time, but then one day it will be the sky and the kiss, and having been loved in the long shadow of liberty.

I get it now. It's really very simple:

That wasn't my baby. That wasn't my husband.

There will be someone. It wasn't him.

Ophelia is looking at the blue sky and she's floated from a patch of cold water to a warmer one. Then something unusual happens. She moves her arms into a backstroke. It's a sunny day and in her head she's listening to Mavis Staples sing "Eyes on the Prize," which goes better with the Velvet Underground than you ever could have guessed. Everywhere Ophelia looks there are prizes to keep her eyes on. These flowers, the way the sun bounces off the boats, even the people waving. She doesn't know where to focus first, but it's a gift.

I can see her from the top deck of the ferry. The water feels good and she turns on her side and, without thinking about it, starts swimming towards the land where she sees this statue, green, arm upstretched, and beneath the statue, tiny but unmistakable, a middle-aged Jewish man with his pants hiked up too high, not the first Jew on Ellis Island, but maybe the smartest, maybe the kindest, maybe, just maybe, the one who changed the most lives. When she gets to land, he isn't there anymore, but she pulls herself up, anyway. She's stronger than anyone knew. Her wet clothes cling to her curves and, as the water ripples out, anyone who saw her from the ferry would not think her broken or damaged, ruined or mad.

But there's no one around for miles, and that makes her happy and calm, as she shakes out her hair.

ACKNOWLEDGMENTS

———————

Thank you:

Felicity Rubinstein. Kim Witherspoon. Elinor Burns. Cliff Roberts.

At Bloomsbury: Alexa von Hirschberg, Anna Simpson, Holly MacDonald, Victoria Millar, Jude Drake, and Alexandra Pringle.

Judith Gurewich and Corinna Barsan at Other Press. Anne Collins and Kylie Barker at Knopf Canada.

For getting through to me and getting me through:

Lisa, Andrea, SB, Teeter, Bianca, Barbara, Shannon, Nat, Sass, Dorothy, Shaye, Maayan, Danielle, Kat, Min, Link, Seamus, Michaela, Shalamar, Asa, Gilah, Elishia, Tendo, Ali, Cleo, Clare, Gary, Indira, Talia, Petra, Lucy, and a special thanks to Rabbi Wolpe.

I'm very grateful to my longtime landlord, Scott, for the Laurel Canyon solitude.

And to: Susan Gelpke-Doran (innkeeper and inspiration)
Not to mention: Sara Hawys Roberts (my girl Friday)

Finally, I'd like to thank the anonymous psychiatrist and author behind the website fxckfeelings.com.